English Skills 2
Answers

Carol Matchett

Schofield & Sims

Which book?

The **English Skills** books are aligned with the end-of-year objectives for Key Stage 2. For the majority of pupils aged seven to 11 years, follow the guidance given on page 2 as to which book to use with each year group.

If a pupil is working significantly above or below the standard normally expected for his or her age, another book may be more appropriate. If you are not sure which to choose, **Workbook descriptors** and a simple **Entry test** are available to help you identify the book that is best suited to the pupil's abilities. You can also use these resources with new pupils joining your class or school.

Photocopy masters of the **Workbook descriptors** and **Entry test** are provided in the **Teacher's Guide** – which also contains the **Entry test marking key**, full instructions for use, and a range of other **English Skills** copymasters. For ordering details, see page 46.

You may be using **English Skills** at Key Stage 3 or with other mixed-ability groups of young people or adults. In such cases you will find the **Workbook descriptors** and **Entry test** vital in deciding which book to give each student.

Published by Schofield & Sims Ltd,
Dogley Mill, Fenay Bridge, Huddersfield HD8 0NQ, UK
Telephone 01484 607080

www.schofieldandsims.co.uk

Copyright © Schofield and Sims Ltd, 2011
Fourth impression 2016

Author: Carol Matchett
Carol Matchett has asserted her moral right under the Copyright, Designs and Patents Act, 1988, to be identified as the author of this work.

British Library Cataloguing in Publication Data
A catalogue record for this book is available from the British Library.

Commissioning and editorial project management by
Carolyn Richardson Publishing Services (www.publiserve.co.uk)

Design by **Ledgard Jepson Ltd**
Printed in the UK by **Wyndeham Grange Ltd**, Southwick, West Sussex

Book 2 Answers ISBN 978 07217 1182 9

Contents Schofield & Sims English Skills 2 Answers

Teacher's notes

Introduction to the series

Schofield & Sims English Skills provides regular and carefully graded practice in key literacy skills. It is designed for use alongside your existing literacy lessons, embedding key aspects of grammar, sentence structure, punctuation and spelling and constantly revisiting them until they become automatic. At the same time it reinforces and develops pupils' knowledge of word structure and vocabulary.

Each workbook comprises three sections with 12 tests in each one. The tests become more difficult, but the increase in difficulty is gradual. The workbooks are fully compatible with the Key Stage 2 literacy curriculum and the final tests in each book are aligned with the end-of-year objectives as follows:

- **Book 1:** Year 2
- **Book 2:** Year 3
- **Book 3:** Year 4
- **Book 4:** Year 5
- **Book 5:** Year 6
- **Book 6:** Years 6/7

Please note: Pupils working towards the objectives for an earlier year should use the appropriate workbook. There is no need for all members of the class to be working on the same book at the same time.

Parts A, B and C

Each test is divided into three parts:

- Part A: **Warm-up** – puzzles, 'warm-up' exercises and revision of earlier learning
- Part B: **Word work** – spelling, word structure, exploring words and their meanings
- Part C: **Sentence work** – putting words together to make sentences: for example, choosing suitable words, forming and punctuating sentences or checking for grammatical accuracy.

Answering the test questions

After you have demonstrated to the class how some of the different question types are to be answered, the pupils work through the test items without adult help – either individually or in pairs. For Books 2 to 6, encourage them to refer to dictionaries, thesauruses and other reference materials rather than asking for your help. The tests may be used flexibly. For example, a test may be tackled in one session or over several days.

Marking

This book provides correct answers for **English Skills 2**; where various different answers would be acceptable, an example is provided. The **Focus** panel stating the areas of learning being tested helps you to decide whether the pupil's answer is satisfactory. **Please note and explain to the class that if all or part of a question has several possible answers, the question number is displayed like this 5 . If a question has a specific answer, the question number is displayed like this 5 . It is displayed in this way even if the answer is made up of several parts that may be given in any order.**

Some questions test more than one area: for example, a question on writing in the past tense might also check pupils' knowledge of the spelling rules for adding **ed**. In such cases, both parts of the answer must be correct, reflecting real-life situations that require varied knowledge and skills.

Group marking sessions

Group or class marking sessions led by the teacher or classroom assistant are the most effective way of marking the tests: pupils learn by comparing and discussing answers.

Another benefit of group or class marking sessions is that they highlight deficits in pupils' knowledge, which will inform your future teaching. Where pupils have given a wrong answer, or none at all, briefly reinforce the key teaching point using an item from this book as a model. In a plenary discussion at the end of the session, encourage pupils to evaluate their own successes; each pupil can then work with a 'talk partner' to record areas needing improvement and discuss appropriate learning objectives.

Suggested questions to ask in a marking session:

- How many different 'correct' answers did we come up with?
- Were some sentence or word choices more interesting or effective than others? Why?
- How do you know this answer is correct?
- How can we make the answer correct?
- Is there an answer that would be even better?
- What are the success criteria for this type of question?
- What are the key points to remember next time?
- When might we put these key points into practice in our reading or writing?

Marking the end-of-section assessments

At the end of each workbook section are two writing assessments: the independent writing task and the proofreading task. These check that pupils are applying in their writing the knowledge, skills and understanding developed in the weekly tests. The assessments also provide evidence of a pupil's strengths and weaknesses, which will help you to set appropriate targets. You might consider sharing with the pupils a simplified version of the mark scheme – and then involve them in setting their own targets, as discussed above.

- *The independent writing task*

The independent writing task gives you a snapshot of a pupil's writing development. Prompts help pupils to plan and gather ideas so that when they begin writing they can focus on expressing their ideas clearly and effectively. On pages 16, 30 and 44 you will find photocopiable **Writing task assessment sheets** – one for each section – with specific assessment points arranged under the headings 'Sentence structure and punctuation', 'Composition and effect' and 'Spelling'. Complete one of these sheets as you mark each pupil's work.

- *The proofreading task*

The proofreading task focuses on punctuation, grammar and spelling. Examples of **Completed proofreading tasks** for each section, also photocopiable, are supplied on pages 17, 31 and 45. However, please note that pupils may choose to correct some of the errors using methods different to those shown in the example but equally valid. For example, two unpunctuated strings of words might be joined using a connective or separated to make two sentences. Additional evidence gained from the relevant proofreading task will help you to further assess pupils' achievements in 'Sentence punctuation' and 'Spelling' as already assessed in the writing task. If you wish, you can use the photocopiable sheet to make notes on a pupil's work.

Please note: Pupils whose scores against the assessment statements are low do not need to repeat a section. All the books revisit difficult areas and offer ample opportunities for further practice. Instead of holding a pupil back, highlight the assessment statements that reveal his or her weaknesses and use these to set learning targets. Ensure that pupils know their targets as they begin the next section.

Progress chart

On page 46 of the pupil workbook only you will find a **Progress chart**, with one column each for Sections 1, 2 and 3, and a list of 'I can' statements relating to the kinds of activities practised in the section. Please ask every pupil to complete the relevant column when they have finished working through a section.

The **Progress chart** encourages pupils to monitor their own work by identifying those activities that they have mastered and those requiring further attention. When pupils colour in the chart as recommended (**green** for **easy, orange** for **getting there** and **red** for **difficult**) it gives a clear picture of progress. It also shows the benefits of systematic practice: an activity that the pupil cannot perform in Section 1 later gets the 'green light'.

The **Progress chart** promotes assessment for learning and personalised learning. Whilst it is best completed in the workbook, so that achievements in all sections may be compared, you may at some point wish to have additional copies. For this reason, it may be photocopied. **However, all other pages of the pupil workbook remain strictly non-photocopiable.**

Section 1 Test 1

A WARM-UP

1 Write a sentence using these words only.

moon the landed The rocket on

The rocket landed on the moon.

Put the letters in order to make two words.

2 **t h e a**   *h e a t*   and   *h a t e*

3 **a e m n**   *m e a n*   and   *n a m e*

Write a question using these words.

4 **bears honey**

When did the bears eat my honey?

5 **trees winter**

Why do trees lose their leaves in winter?

Add the missing letters.   ***Clue: days of the week***

6 M _o_ n d _a_ y

7 S _a_ t u r d _a_ y

8 W _e_ d n _e_ s d _a_ y

9 T h _u_ r s d _a_ y

10 T _u_ e s d _a_ y

> **PART A Focus**
> **1:** sentence formation
> **2–3:** visual spelling strategy
> **4–5:** forming questions; adding question marks
> **6–10:** syllables; high-frequency words

B WORD WORK

Write two compound words starting with **some**.

1 some *time*

2 some *thing*

Write three words that mean the same as the word in **bold**.

3 **little** house   *small*   *tiny*   *miniscule*

4 I was **happy.**   *joyful*   *pleased*   *cheerful*

Underline the word that is wrongly spelt. Write the correct spelling.

5 The King <u>frownd</u>.   *frowned*

6 The crowd <u>gaspt</u>.   *gasped*

7 Clouds <u>floatid</u> by.   *floated*

Add the missing syllable.

8 l e m _on_ a d e

9 d i _no_ s a u r

10 h e l i _cop_ t e r

> **PART B Focus**
> **1–2:** compound words
> **3–4:** synonyms; choosing adjectives
> **5–7:** identifying common errors; adding ed to verbs
> **8–10:** using syllables to spell longer words

C SENTENCE WORK

1 Write this message without using the word **and**.

We went to the city farm and we saw a baby lamb and he was lovely.

We went to the city farm. We saw a baby lamb. He was lovely.

2 Circle the four capital letters.   On Saturday I saw Molly in town.

Write down why the capital letter was used.

3 O: *It's at the beginning of the sentence.*

4 S: *Saturday is the name of a day of the week.*

5 I: *The word I is always a capital letter.*

6 M: *Molly is a person's name.*

Use the words to make a question.

7 Jack did win.   *Did Jack win?*

8 I can do that.   *Can I do that?*

9 They will come.   *Will they come?*

10 You must go.   *Must you go?*

> **PART C Focus**
> **1:** writing separate sentences
> **2–6:** using capital letters
> **7–10:** forming questions; changing punctuation

4   X DEFINITIVE ANSWER   X SAMPLE ANSWER

Section 1 Test 2

A WARM-UP

1 Write a sentence using these words.

dog duck

The dog barked at the duck.

Use these words to make four compound words.

spoon pot cake pan tea dust

2 teaspoon   **4** pancake

3 dustpan   **5** teacake

Write the pairs of words that rhyme.
Add another word to each pair.

snail great day whale grey late

6 snail , whale and tail

7 great , late   and plate

8 day   , grey   and play

> **PART A**
> Focus
> **1&9:** sentence formation and punctuation
> **2–5:** compound words
> **6–8:** vowel phoneme **ai**
> **10:** question formation

9 Put these words in order to make a sentence.

you I that help with can

I can help you with that.

10 Make a question using the same words.

Can I help you with that?

B WORD WORK

Add the correct plural ending.

1 short _s_

2 jean _s_

3 sunglass _es_

Write the meaning of the word in **bold**.

4 The monster's face was **hideous**.

'hideous' means ugly

5 The water **glistened** in the sun.

'glistened' means sparkled

6 The car had been **abandoned**.

'abandoned' means dumped

Write four words that start with **ph**.

7 ph otograph

8 ph one

9 ph rase

10 ph onics

> **PART B Focus**
> **1–3:** plural endings s and es
> **4–6:** inferring word meanings from context
> **7–10:** using the grapheme **ph**

C SENTENCE WORK

What punctuation mark is hidden by the symbol?

I have my pencil■ ruler■ crayons and book▲

1 ▲ is a full stop (.)

2 ■ is a comma (,)

> **PART C Focus**
> **1–3:** using commas and full stops
> **4–6:** varying sentences; choosing appropriate nouns
> **7–10:** checking grammatical accuracy and punctuation

3 Add four items to complete the sentence.

I went shopping and I bought bread, cakes, milk and apples.

Change the words in **bold** to make a new sentence. Write the new sentence.

4 A **cloud** floated in the **sky**.   A toy boat floated in the water.

5 **James** dropped the **jelly**.   Dad dropped the marmalade.

6 A **cat** crept through the **grass**.   A tiger crept through the jungle.

Write the sentence correctly.

7 he goed home   He went home.

8 she must of lost it She must have lost it.

9 we was in a hurry We were in a hurry.

10 were are you   Where are you?

Section 1 Test 3

A WARM-UP

1 Write a sentence using these words only.

shook the girl her head little

The little girl shook her head.

The same vowel sound is missing from all these words. Write it in.

2 s t _or_ m   **4** c _or_ n

3 l _or_ d   **5** t _or_ c h

Write two more words with the same spelling of the vowel sound.

6 porch

7 morning

> **PART A Focus**
> **1:** forming sentences
> **2–7:** blending vowel phonemes
> **8–9:** spelling patterns
> **10:** forming questions

Write the pairs of words with the same spelling pattern. Add another rhyming word.

brother would another could

8 brother , another and mother

9 could , would and should

10 Write a question with these words in it.

elephant trunk

How does an elephant use its trunk?

B WORD WORK

Underline the correct spelling.

1 peeple peopel <u>people</u> peepul

2 tippt <u>tipped</u> tiped tipt

3 dishis <u>dishes</u> dishs dishies

Write two words that mean the same as the word in **bold**.

4 **cold**   freezing   chilly

5 **fast**   speedy   quick

6 **old**   ancient   aged

7 **sad**   miserable   gloomy

Write three words that start with **ch** when it sounds as it does in the name **Chris**.

8 character

9 chemist

10 chorus

> **PART B Focus**
> **1–3:** common spelling errors
> **4–7:** synonyms for common words
> **8–10:** alternative pronunciation for **ch**

C SENTENCE WORK

Read this aloud.   **the rain poured down everyone was soaked the picnic was ruined**

1 How many sentences did you hear?   three

2 Write the sentences with full stops and capital letters.

The rain poured down. Everyone was soaked. The picnic was ruined.

Add **but** or **so**.

3 He found the door _but_ it was locked.   **5** It is cold _but_ it is not raining.

4 He found the door _so_ he could escape.   **6** It is cold _so_ wrap up warm.

Write the sentence in the past tense.

7 This week, we go on holiday. Last week, we went on holiday .

8 Today it rains. Yesterday it rained .

9 The dragon snarls. Then the dragon snarled .

10 Complete the sentence and add any punctuation marks that are missing.

Inside the chest there was a magic mirror, thirty coins, a string of beads and a treasure map.

> **PART C Focus**
> **1–2:** punctuating sentences
> **3–6:** forming compound sentences
> **7–9:** using past tense; verbs ending with **ed**
> **10:** completing sentences; using commas in a list

A WARM-UP

Write six sentences using these words only.
Use three words in each sentence.

he we they was were happy cold

1. He was happy.
2. He was cold.
3. We were happy.
4. We were cold.
5. They were happy.
6. They were cold.

Make two four-letter words using these letters only.

7. **r d a e**   read   and   dare
8. **a e r t**   rate   and   tear

Use these words to make two compound words.

fly green house

9. greenfly
10. greenhouse

> **PART A Focus**
> **1–6:** grammatical agreement; sentence punctuation
> **7–8:** visual spelling strategy
> **9–10:** compound words

B WORD WORK

Add the missing syllable.   *Clue: colours*

1. s c a r _let_   3. e m _er_ a l d
2. b u r _gun_ d y   4. v i _o_ l e t

5. The same letter is missing from all these words. Write it in.

   w _a_ s h   w _a_ n t   w _a_ s

> **PART B Focus**
> **1–4:** using syllables for spelling
> **5:** wa spelling
> **6–8:** working out meaning; technical words
> **9–10:** common errors; high-frequency words

Write the meaning of the word in **bold**.

6. a woodland **habitat**
   a 'habitat' is a home or environment

7. Flowers **produce** seeds.
   'produce' means make or create

8. Fruit **contains** seeds.
   'contains' means holds or has inside

Underline the word that is wrongly spelt. Write the correct spelling.

9. It was abowt five o'clock.   about
10. The howse seemed empty.   house

C SENTENCE WORK

Add the missing punctuation and capital letters.

1. I watched the match last night. Did you see it?
2. Ben, Ella, Samir, Megan and Sarika were in my group.
3. Did you hear about Ryan? He broke his arm.

> **PART C Focus**
> **1–3:** proofreading for punctuation
> **4–6:** irregular past tense verbs
> **7–9:** extending simple sentences
> **10:** turning notes into a full sentence

Cross out the word that is wrong. Write it correctly.

4. I ~~woked~~ up early today.   woke
5. The wind ~~blowed~~.   blew
6. We all ~~weared~~ our PE kit.   wore

Add to these sentences to say **where** each event happened.

7. We saw the car outside the bank.
8. A plane landed in the playground.
9. The man hid behind the tree.

10. Write the notes as one complete sentence.

    tadpole – young frog   A tadpole is a young frog.

X DEFINITIVE ANSWER   X SAMPLE ANSWER

Section 1 Test 5

A WARM-UP

Write a sentence using these words.

1 dog roof

The dog was barking at someone

on the roof.

2 Gran sunglasses

Gran lost her sunglasses

on the beach.

3 animal motorway

An animal was walking along

the motorway.

Add the missing letters. **ir er ur or**

4 b _ir_ d

5 c h _ur_ c h

6 w _or_ k

7 h _er_ b

Make three questions.

8 *What* is your name **?**

9 *Where* do you live **?**

10 *How* old are you **?**

> **PART A Focus**
> **1–3:** forming and punctuating sentences
> **4–7:** different spellings of the phoneme ur
> **8–10:** forming and punctuating questions

B WORD WORK

Make six words using these words and prefixes only.

able like please un dis well

Write the word beside its meaning.

1	*unwell*	ill or sick
2	*displease*	annoy or upset
3	*disable*	put out of action
4	*dislike*	hate
5	*unable*	not able to do something
6	*unlike*	different

Underline the correct spelling.

7 brushis <u>brushes</u> brushs

8 wishis wishs <u>wishes</u>

> **PART B Focus**
> **1–6:** adding prefixes to make words; word meanings
> **7–8:** adding **es** to form plurals
> **9–10:** spelling pattern **le**

These words have the same spelling pattern.

giggle puddle wobble drizzle

9 What is the pattern?

Double letters are followed by

an 'le' ending.

10 Write two more words with this pattern.

bubble *apple*

C SENTENCE WORK

1 Add three items.   **In my sandwich I had** *cheese, lettuce and tomato.*

Write an ending for the sentence.

2 **We left early but** *still arrived late for school.*

3 **We left early so** *we had lots of time.*

Underline the verb.

4 Lizards <u>eat</u> insects.

5 Tigers <u>hunt</u> at night.

6 Hummingbirds <u>hover</u> near flowers.

7 Chimps <u>swing</u> through trees.

Add capital letters and full stops.

8 ᵀthe wind turned icy ᴸlucy shivered ˢshe hated the cold.

9 ᴵit was getting late ᴹmr ᴮbrown frowned and looked at his watch.

10 ᴹmark lay in bed ᴴhe listened for a moment ᴵit all seemed quiet

> **PART C Focus**
> **1:** commas between items in a list
> **2–3:** forming compound sentences
> **4–7:** identifying verbs
> **8–10:** identifying and demarcating sentence boundaries

X **DEFINITIVE ANSWER**   X **SAMPLE ANSWER**

Section 1   Test 6

Put the words into rhyming pairs.
Add another word to each pair.

stair fear door peer more bear

1	_stair_	,	_bear_	and	_fair_
2	_fear_	,	_peer_	and	_here_
3	_door_	,	_more_	and	_for_

4 Change the words in **bold** to make a new sentence.

Butter is made from **cream**.

Bread is made from _flour_ .

Make six sentences using some of these words only.

I she we is are am brave late

5 I am brave.
6 I am late.
7 She is brave.
8 She is late.
9 We are brave.
10 We are late.

PART A Focus
1–3: rhyme; alternative spellings of vowel phonemes
4: sentence variation; nouns; making sense.
5–10: grammatical agreement; sentence punctuation

B   WORD WORK

Write these verbs so they end with **ing**.

1	drum _ming_	4	whirl _ing_
2	hook _ing_	5	bob _bing_
3	spit _ting_	6	hear _ing_

Write these sentences with all the words spelt correctly.

7 We wotcht the swons and swollows.

We watched the swans and swallows.

8 She pickt up the boxis foor him.

She picked up the boxes for him.

Sort the verbs into two groups.

amble   dart   dash   plod
trudge   sprint   saunter   tear

| 9 | **run** | _sprint, dart, dash, tear_ |
| 10 | **walk** | _plod, trudge, saunter, amble_ |

PART B Focus
1–6: double letter rule when adding **ing**
7–8: correcting spelling errors
9–10: alternatives for high-frequency verbs

C   SENTENCE WORK

Write a sentence using these words.

1	**bark and cat**	_The dog began to bark and the cat ran away._
2	**home but road**	_They wanted to go home but they could not find the right road._
3	**gold but cave**	_The gold was hidden somewhere but it was not in the cave._

Add a verb.

4 The man _disappeared_ in a puff of smoke.
5 They all _lived_ happily ever after.
6 The door _sprang_ open.

PART C Focus
1–3: forming and punctuating compound sentences
4–6: selecting verbs
7–8: correcting grammatical and punctuation errors in sentences
9–10: understanding sentences

Write the sentence correctly.

7 **the giant strided over the hill**

The giant strode over the hill.

8 **someone must of lost it**

Someone must have lost it.

9 Is this a sentence? **The little grey rabbit.**

_No_

10 Give a reason for your answer.

It is not complete. It has no verb.

| X DEFINITIVE ANSWER | X SAMPLE ANSWER |

9

Section 1 Test 7

A WARM-UP

1 All the words have the same letters missing. Write them in.

ar er or ir ur

w _or_ t h   w _or_ s e

w _or_ k   w _or_ l d

Write a question using these words only.

2 **is it dark night why at**

Why is it dark at night?

3 **fizzy lemonade is why**

Why is lemonade fizzy?

Add **un** or **dis** to make a new word.

4 _dis_ t r u s t   **6** _un_ s e l f i s h

5 _un_ h a p p y   **7** _dis_ a g r e e

Add the missing letters.

Clue: found in the garden

8 b u t t _e_ r f l y

9 d a n d _e_ l _i_ o n

10 c a _t_ e r p _i_ l l _a_ r

PART A Focus
1: wor spelling pattern
2–3: forming questions
4–7: common prefixes
8–10: spelling longer words

B WORD WORK

1 Underline the three words that mean the same as **looked**.

<u>glanced</u> <u>glared</u> nudged <u>peered</u> jerked

Add another word to make a compound word.

2 farm _yard_

3 snow _flake_

4 play _time_

PART B Focus
1: synonyms for common verbs
2–4: compound words
5–8: plural spelling rules –
adding s or **es**
9–10: common suffixes

Make the noun into a plural.

5 one dish   → three _dishes_

6 one plate   → three _plates_

7 one lunchbox → three _lunchboxes_

8 one glass   → three _glasses_

Add the same suffix to all three words.

9 hope _ful_   pain _ful_   wish _ful_

10 smooth _ly_   kind _ly_   sudden _ly_

C SENTENCE WORK

Cross out the verb and write one of these instead.

collapsed swaggered heaved

1 He ~~put~~ the sack onto his back.   _heaved_

2 The bridge ~~fell~~.   _collapsed_

3 The pirate ~~went~~ down the road.   _swaggered_

Add a question mark or an exclamation mark to the end of the book title.

4 Look out _!_

5 Oh no, Joe _!_

6 Why does the wind blow _?_

7 Can I _?_

8 Whose shoes _?_

9 Stop thief _!_

10 Complete this sentence.

Plants have roots so _they can take in water._

PART C Focus
1–3: selecting precise verbs suitable for context
4–9: demarcating questions and exclamations
10: forming a sentence using so

X DEFINITIVE ANSWER   X SAMPLE ANSWER

A WARM-UP

1 Change the words in **bold** to make a new sentence.

All elephants have trunks.

All birds have beaks.

> **PART A Focus**
> **1:** sentence variation; changing nouns
> **2–5:** high-frequency words
> **6–9:** adding suffixes
> **10:** writing linked sentences

Add the missing letters. **Clue: months**

2 N o v e m b e r
3 S e p t e m b e r
4 J a n u a r y
5 F e b r u a r y

Make four new words out of these words and suffixes.

ly ful fear power

6 fearful
7 fearfully
8 powerful
9 powerfully

10 Write two sentences. Use one of these words in each.

cake mess

Danny dropped the cake on the floor.

It made a real mess on the carpet.

B WORD WORK

Write the meaning of the word in **bold**.

1 Suddenly someone **yanked** my arm.

'yanked' means pulled

2 The King was well **protected**.

'protected' means guarded

Cross out the words that are wrongly spelt. Write the correct spellings.

3 Her dad ~~werks~~ all over the ~~world~~.

works   world

4 Use the ~~handel~~ to lift the ~~kettel~~.

handle   kettle

5 He ~~startid~~ to ~~wosh~~ the ~~dishis~~.

started   wash   dishes

Write the verb with the **ed** ending added.

6 **train** trained
7 **trot** trotted
8 **snap** snapped
9 **tap** tapped
10 **leap** leaped

> **PART B Focus**
> **1–2:** inferring meaning
> **3–5:** common spelling errors
> **6–10:** adding ed to verbs; the double letter rule

C SENTENCE WORK

Write a noun in each space to complete the sentence.

1 Three ___hens___ were sitting on the old ___tractor___ by the ___barn___ in the farmyard.

2 From the beach we could see fishing boats bobbing in the ___sea___ near the ___harbour___ .

3 In the supermarket, a ___customer___ with a ___trolley___ was standing by the ___checkout___ .

Write the sentence as a short exclamation.

4 I need some help. Help!

5 I think he will go bananas. He'll go bananas!

6 Suddenly there was a crash. CRASH!

Add the capital letters.

7 on saturday i went to see manchester city play aston villa.

8 on sunday i went to simeon's house in west burton.

Complete the sentence.

9 Ice-cream starts to melt when it gets hot.

10 Water freezes when it is very cold.

> **PART C Focus**
> **1–3:** choosing nouns to fit the setting and the sentence
> **4–6:** exclamations and exclamation marks
> **7–8:** using capital letters
> **9–10:** forming sentences using **when** to explain

Section 1   Test 9

A   WARM-UP

Use the letters to make two words.

1. **a e c r**   _race_ and _care_
2. **e o r s**   _rose_ and _sore_

3. Write a sentence using these words.

cupboard but empty

The lady opened the cupboard but
to her surprise it was empty.

4. Add four nouns to complete the sentence.

In the garden we saw beetles, _bees,_
butterflies, caterpillars and snails.

Make four compound words ending with **room**.

5. _bedroom_   7. _classroom_
6. _cloakroom_   8. _stockroom_

Add the missing letters.

9. O n c e u p o n a t i m e
10. H a p p i l y e v e r a f t e r

> **PART A Focus**
> **1–2:** visual spelling skills; modifying e
> **3:** compound sentences using **but**
> **4:** commas in a list; plural spellings
> **5–8:** compound words
> **9–10:** spelling of story phrases

B   WORD WORK

1. What spelling rule do these words follow?

snagged spinning spotted dragging

If a verb has a short vowel
before the last letter, double
the letter to add 'ing' or 'ed'.

Give two more examples.

2. _swimming_   3. _hopped_

> **PART B Focus**
> **1–3:** rules for adding ing, ed
> **4–7:** precise nouns
> **8–10:** meaning of prefixes

Write three nouns that name types of

4. **shop** _newsagent_ , _bakers_ , _chemist_
5. **road vehicle** _van_ , _lorry_ , _tractor_
6. **dog** _dalmation_ , _greyhound_ , _spaniel_
7. **sportswear** _trainers_ , _leotard_ , _shorts_

Add the correct prefix. Then write the meaning of the new word.

un dis non

8. _dis_ **trust**   means _not to believe_
9. _non_ **sense**   means _without meaning_
10. _un_ **popular** means _not liked_

C   SENTENCE WORK

Cross out the word **came** and use one of these words instead.

swarmed slithered trickled

1. Water ~~came~~ out of the pipe.   _trickled_
2. The ants ~~came~~ out of the hole.   _swarmed_
3. The snake ~~came~~ across the floor. _slithered_

> **PART C Focus**
> **1–3:** verbs for precision and impact
> **4–8:** question and exclamation marks
> **9–10:** giving reasons following **because**

Add the correct punctuation mark at the end of the line.

4. **Mum:** Shall we have beans for tea _?_
5. **Child:** NO _!_
6. **Mum:** But you like beans on toast _._
7. **Child:** NO _!_
8. **Mum:** Well, what about spaghetti then _?_

Finish the sentence.

9. Goldilocks ran away because _she was frightened by the three bears._
10. Little Bear was angry because _Goldilocks had broken his chair._

12   X DEFINITIVE ANSWER   X SAMPLE ANSWER

A   WARM-UP

Put the words into rhyming pairs.
Add another rhyming word.

burn moon born prune learn lawn

1   _burn_   ,   _learn_   and   _stern_
2   _moon_   ,   _prune_   and   _spoon_
3   _born_   ,   _lawn_   and   _thorn_

Write a sentence, a question and an exclamation
using the word **spaceship**.

4   **sentence**   _We saw a spaceship_
in the sky last night.

5   **question**   _Was that a spaceship?_

6   **exclamation**   _Wow, a spaceship!_

> **PART A Focus**
> **1–3:** different spellings of vowel phonemes
> **4–6:** forming different types of sentence
> **7–10:** high-frequency words

Add the missing vowels.

Clue: numbers

7   s e v e n t e e n
8   f o u r t e e n
9   e l e v e n
10   e i g h t e e n

B   WORD WORK

Add to each sentence a verb ending with **ing**.

1   Ducks were ___splashing___ about
on the water.

2   Ed was ___dragging___ the branch
behind him.

3   The man is ___nodding___ his head
in agreement.

4   I felt you ___tapping___ my shoulder.

Add the missing letters.

> **PART B Focus**
> **1–4:** selecting suitable verbs; rules for adding **ing**
> **5–7:** vowel phonemes; compound words
> **8–10:** choosing precise verbs; using a thesaurus

5   g r e e n h o u s e
6   p l a y g r o u n d
7   l i g h t h o u s e

Write two words to use instead of **said** which could
show that a person was

8   **speaking loudly**   _shouted_   _screamed_
9   **speaking quietly**   _whispered_   _sighed_
10   **speaking happily**   _laughed_   _chuckled_

C   SENTENCE WORK

Use one of these nouns in place of the crossed-out word.

office cottage theatre palace

1   The King waited in his ~~house~~.   _palace_

2   The fisherman waited in his ~~house~~.   _cottage_

3   The businessman hurried into the ~~building~~.   _office_

4   The actor hurried into the ~~building~~.   _theatre_

> **PART C Focus**
> **1–4:** precise nouns
> **5–7:** using connectives to form longer sentences
> **8–10:** proofreading for punctuation

Finish the sentence.

5   The post office was closed when _we got there._

6   The post office was closed so _we could not post the parcel._

7   The post office was closed because _it was after six o'clock._

Add the capital letters and punctuation.

8   It began to snow. Soft flakes gently landed on Sarah's hair.

9   Suddenly there was a loud sound. Boom! What was it?

10   What is your favourite sort of dog? Is it a poodle, a greyhound, a collie or a bulldog?

Section 1   Test 11

A   WARM-UP

Finish the sentence.

1   Dogs bark when *they hear a noise.*

2   I feel happy when *the sun shines.*

Read the words aloud. Underline the odd one out.

3   hear   beard   <u>bear</u>   near

4   Give a reason for your choice.

The letters 'ear' make a different

sound in this word.

Add the missing syllable.   **Clue: sports**

5   a t h *let* i c s

6   b a d *min* t o n

7   g y m *nas* t i c s

8   s w i m *ming*

> **PART A Focus**
> **1–2:** using the connective when
> **3–4:** different pronunciations of graphemes
> **5–8:** using syllables in spelling
> **9–10:** forming sentences and questions

Write a sentence and a question using these words only.

swim can bears polar

9   **sentence**   *Polar bears can swim.*

10   **question**   *Can polar bears swim?*

B   WORD WORK

1   What spelling rule do these words follow?

dishes passes fizzes matches

Add 'es' to words ending with a hissing

or buzzing sound.

Write two more words that follow the same rule.

2   *wishes*   3   *patches*

4   The same letter is missing from all these words. Write it in.

s w *a* l l o w   s w *a* p   w *a* n d e r

Write two verbs that mean the same as

5   **jump**   *leap*   *bound*

6   **shine**   *glow*   *gleam*

Add a prefix and a suffix.

un dis ful ly

7   *un* fair *ly*

8   *un* like *ly*

9   *un* help *ful*

10   *dis* trust *ful*

> **PART B Focus**
> **1–3:** plurals where es is added
> **4:** wa spelling pattern
> **5–6:** synonyms for common verbs; using a thesaurus
> **7–10:** adding prefixes and suffixes

C   SENTENCE WORK

Add a word to complete the sentence.

hunted hurled hurtled huddled

1   Adam   *hurled*   his toys away.

2   Our dog Ziggy   *hurtled*   into the lake.

3   Lucy   *huddled*   by the fire to keep warm.

4   Deepak   *hunted*   for his rucksack.

> **PART C Focus**
> **1–4:** choosing verbs for impact
> **5–7:** using precise nouns
> **8–10:** proofreading, checking for grammar and punctuation errors

Underline the nouns.

5   The <u>boys</u> packed <u>tents</u>, <u>sleeping bags</u> and a powerful <u>torch</u>.

6   What do these words tell us about what the boys are going to do?   *They are going camping.*

7   Change the nouns to make a new sentence.

The   *family*   packed   *sandwiches, a flask of tea and a picnic rug.*

Write the sentence/s correctly.

8   **Nina tom and sacha lives in george street**   *Nina, Tom and Sacha live in George Street.*

9   **I red two book last week what about you**   *I read two books last week. What about you?*

10   **He were late he must of misst the bus**   *He was late. He must have missed the bus.*

X DEFINITIVE ANSWER   X SAMPLE ANSWER

Section 1 Test 12

A WARM-UP

Add a word to complete the sentence.

1 The car ___stopped___ suddenly.

2 Everyone ___sang___ happily.

3 The same phoneme is missing from all these words. Write it in.

f _ar_ m e r   h _ar_ m f u l   g _ar_ d e n

Add a prefix and a suffix.

4 _un_ **fair** _ly_   _un_ **grate** _ful_

5 Look at how these words end. Underline the odd one out.

double   label   table   bubble

6 Give a reason for your choice.

It ends with 'el' rather than 'le'.

Write four compound words that start with **sun**.

7 sunshine   9 sunbathe

8 sunburn   10 sunflower

> **PART A Focus**
> **1–2:** adding suitable verbs
> **3:** the phoneme **ar**
> **4:** prefixes and suffixes
> **5–6:** the **le** ending
> **7–10:** compound words; using a dictionary

B WORD WORK

Write the meaning of the word in **bold**.

1 It was not what he **intended**.

'intended' means planned

2 She was **irritated** by my remark.

'irritated' means annoyed

3 He **trudged** back up the hill.

'trudged' means walked slowly

Add **un** or **dis** to make new verbs.

4 _dis_ **own**   6 _un_ **tie**

5 _un_ **fold**   7 _dis_ **infect**

> **PART B Focus**
> **1–3:** inferring meaning
> **4–7:** adding the prefixes **dis** and **un**
> **8–10:** adding **ing** to words ending with **e**

8 What spelling rule do these words follow?

baking striding sparkling

Drop the final 'e' to add 'ing'.

Write two more examples of words following this rule.

9 taking   10 hiding

C SENTENCE WORK

1 Underline the nouns in the sentence below.

2 Then draw a ring round the verbs.

The seagulls (squawked) loudly as the waves (crept) across the sand.

3 What setting does the sentence describe? the seaside

Change the nouns and verbs so that the sentence describes

4 **a wood** The ___owl hooted___ loudly as the ___wind rushed___ across the ___tree tops___.

5 **a street** The ___car engines growled___ loudly as the ___shoppers struggled___ across the ___road___.

> **PART C Focus**
> **1–5:** precise nouns and verbs
> **6–8:** time relationships; adding another part to a sentence
> **9–10:** compound sentences containing contrasting information

Finish the sentence by adding words that say **when** the event happened.

6 Kerry woke up early the next morning.

7 They ran outside to play as soon as it stopped raining.

8 We piled into the car straight after breakfast.

Write the notes as a complete sentence.

9 **all birds – wings   not all fly** All birds have wings but they do not all fly.

10 **Monday – sunny   Tuesday – rain** On Monday it was sunny but on Tuesday it rained.

Remind the pupil to complete Section 1 of the Progress chart on page 46 of the workbook.

Schofield & Sims English Skills 2

Section 1 Writing task assessment sheet: Sam gets lost

Name		Class/Set
Teacher's name		Date

Sentence structure and punctuation

	Always/often	Sometimes	Never
Writes in complete sentences			
Uses compound and simple sentences			
Uses connectives to extend sentences (e.g., **because**, **when**)			
Demarcates sentences accurately			
Uses commas in a list			
Maintains use of past tense			
Maintains use of third person			
Grammatical agreement correct			

Composition and effect

Writing sounds like a story			
The event is developed and expanded through description and/or detail			
Character's feelings are described			
Time-related words and phrases used to link events			
Nouns (e.g., those relating to setting) are chosen for precision			
Verbs are chosen for clarity and interest (e.g., describing sounds, actions)			

Spelling

Words with regular vowel phonemes spelt correctly			
Compound words or words with phonically regular syllables spelt correctly			
High-frequency words spelt correctly			
Any words using prefixes (**un**, **dis**) or suffixes (**ful**, **ly**) spelt correctly			
Verb endings (**ing** and **ed**) used correctly, with doubling of final consonant			
Spelling of plurals correct			

Writing task summary

Schofield & Sims English Skills 2

Section 1 Completed proofreading task: My camping diary

Name	Class/Set
Teacher's name	Date

W   ed   Saturday   B A

we arrivd at camp on sataday. I was shareing a tent with ben, adam and Harvey.

because   was

Mick was unnable to come. becuwse he were not well.

First   learn   W watched M J   demon

Furst we had to lern how to put up our tent. we wotcht mr jenkins demastrate

A   ph   l

and then we had a go. adam took a foto off us when the tent was finaly up.

ed   in W   because

It was just then that it startid to rayn. we all huddeled in our tent the

in   I was getting o   o I   drumming

rayn kept comeing. it were geting werse and werse. it was druming on the canvas

S

and there was a huge puddel of warter forming on the roof of the tent. suddenley

g   ped   d   W were   soaked!

somethink snapt and the tent collapset on top of us. we was all sowkt

Proofreading task summary

Section 1 tasks summary

Section 2 Test 1

A WARM-UP

Write two sentences for a story. Use one of these nouns in each sentence.

farmer   tree

1   *The farmer found a place to rest.*
2   *He lay down under a tall tree.*

3   Underline the odd one out.   *Clue: spelling*

<u>hissing</u>   stepping   nodding   thudding

4   Give a reason for your choice.

'Hiss' has a double letter already,
before you add 'ing'.

5   Cross out the nouns. Write new nouns.

~~Smoke~~ drifted in the ~~air~~.   *Clouds*   *sky*

Write three compound words ending with **thing**.

6   *some* thing
7   *no* thing
8   *every* thing

> **PART A Focus**
> **1–2:** writing linked sentences for a story
> **3–4:** doubling last letter before ing
> **5:** choosing nouns
> **6–8:** high-frequency compound words
> **9–10:** rhyming words; **are** and **eer** graphemes

Add the missing phoneme to make two rhyming words. **are   eer**

9   g l *are*   and   s t *are*
10   c h *eer*   and   j *eer*

B WORD WORK

These words and prefixes are mixed up. Write them correctly.

unbehave **mis**obey **im**lucky **dis**possible

1   *misbehave*   3   *impossible*
2   *unlucky*   4   *disobey*

5   How do the prefixes change the meanings of the words?

They make them into opposites.

6   What spelling rule do these words follow?

spies teddies parties

In words ending with a consonant
then a 'y', change 'y' to 'i' before
adding 'es'.

7   Write another word that follows the same rule.

flies

> **PART B Focus**
> **1–5:** understanding prefixes
> **6–7:** plural spelling rule for words ending with y
> **8–10:** topic words (settlements); using a dictionary

Write the meaning of the word in **bold**.

8   **settlement**   *place where people live*
9   **population**   *people who live there*
10   **occupation**   *job*

C SENTENCE WORK

Add the connecting word.

while   until   after   since

1   Jack was glad to be home *after* his adventure.
2   Someone had broken in *while* they were out.
3   They walked *until* they could go no further.
4   Jason had been an unusual child *since* birth.

Underline the verb and change it to the present tense.

5   Leo <u>lived</u> on a far away island.   *lives*
6   Something <u>tapped</u> on the window.   *taps*
7   Emma and Lucy <u>were</u> friends.   *are*

Add the capital letters.

8   F̶lorence N̶ightingale was born in F̶lorence in I̶taly.
9   T̶urn left into P̶ark S̶treet at S̶immond's S̶upermarket.
10   I̶ enjoyed 'S̶nip S̶nap', which is the new book by S̶am J̶ackson.

> **PART C Focus**
> **1–4:** using connectives/connecting words within sentences
> **5–7:** identifying verbs; past and present tense forms
> **8–10:** using capital letters

X **DEFINITIVE ANSWER**   X **SAMPLE ANSWER**

Section 2 Test 2

A WARM-UP

1 Change the first part of the sentence.

~~The wind howled~~ but I was safe in the hut.

The lion roared

2 Write a sentence using these words.

milk but cat

I looked for the milk but the cat
had drunk it.

3 The same phoneme is missing from all these words. Write it in.

bef _ore_   m _ore_   sh _ore_ line

Add the missing syllable to complete the list of rhyming words.

4 tum _ble_   grum _ble_   rum _ble_
5 mud _dle_   pud _dle_   cud _dle_
6 bub _ble_   trou _ble_   stub _ble_

Add a word to make a compound word.

7 luke _warm_   **9** draw _bridge_
8 wheel _chair_   **10** horse _shoe_

PART A Focus
1–2: forming compound sentences
3: ore spelling
4–6: le spelling pattern
7–10: compound words; using a dictionary

B WORD WORK

Underline the correct plural spelling.

1 <u>donkeys</u> donkies donkyes
2 puppys <u>puppies</u> puppyes
3 witchis witchies <u>witches</u>

Underline the suffix that you can add to all the words. Write it in.

4 ly <u>est</u> ful
quick _est_   long _est_   kind _est_

5 ful <u>less</u> ly
care _less_   end _less_   friend _less_

6 ly less <u>er</u>
rich _er_   kind _er_   tall _er_

PART B Focus
1–3: plural spelling rules
4–6: suffixes
7–10: choosing synonyms; using a thesaurus

Synonyms are words with similar meanings. Write two synonyms for the word in **bold**.

7 a **silly** idea   foolish   ridiculous
8 a **fierce** beast   savage   vicious
9 the **moody** boy   sulky   sullen
10 a **bright** light   glowing   brilliant

C SENTENCE WORK

Cross out the nouns. Write new nouns to make the sentence more interesting.

1 A ~~man~~ rode a ~~bike~~ along the ~~road~~.   clown   unicycle   tightrope
2 The ~~dog~~ jumped from the ~~wall~~ into the ~~bush~~.   man   helicopter   sea
3 The ~~woman~~ took the ~~dog~~ to the ~~shop~~.   lady   children   seaside
4 The ~~boy~~ crossed the ~~road~~ to reach the ~~shop~~.   ship   sea   island

Add more to each instruction so it says exactly **where**.

5 Sieve the flour _into a bowl._
6 Bake the pie _in a hot oven._
7 Sprinkle sugar _over the top of the cake._

What punctuation mark is hidden by the symbol?

▲We need biscuits■ eggs■ cereal and milk■ ▼ said Mum◆

8 ▲ ▼ = _speech marks_
9 ■ = _commas_
10 ◆ = _full stop_

PART C Focus
1–4: nouns for precision and interest
5–7: extending simple sentences to add precision
8–10: using punctuation

X DEFINITIVE ANSWER   X SAMPLE ANSWER   **19**

Section 2 Test 3

A WARM-UP

The beginnings and endings of these sentences are mixed up.

All books	**is fiction.**
Some books	**have pages.**
A storybook	**has a glossary.**
This book	**are non-fiction.**

> **PART A Focus**
> **1–4:** grammatical agreement
> **5–8:** compound words; topic words (clothing)
> **9–10:** visual spelling skills

Write the sentences correctly.

1. All books have pages.
2. Some books are non-fiction.
3. A storybook is fiction.
4. This book has a glossary.

Make four compound words. *Clue: clothing*

suit sweat over pull track coat shirt

5. tracksuit
7. sweatshirt
6. overcoat
8. pullover

Use the letters to make a different word.

9. **t h i n g** n i g h t
10. **n o w** w o n

B WORD WORK

Write the phrase so that the verb ends with **ing** and the noun is plural.

1. make jelly making jellies
2. drop catch dropping catches
3. smile face smiling faces

4. Add a prefix to make an opposite.

un tidy   dis honest
in visible   de bug

Use the words in these sentences.

> **PART B Focus**
> **1–3:** applying spelling rules
> **4–8:** prefixes; word meanings
> **9–10:** inferring meaning; using a dictionary

5. This room is untidy .
6. He had a dishonest face.
7. The wizard made himself invisible .
8. We had to debug the computer.

Write the meaning of the word in **bold**.

9. It was an **enchanting** evening.
   'enchanting' means delightful
10. He had to **obey** the King's wishes.
    'obey' means do as you are told

C SENTENCE WORK

Add capital letters and full stops.

1. <u>A</u> a fish is an animal with a tail and fins. <u>I</u> it lives in water.
2. <u>G</u> gently heat the mixture. <u>A</u> add the fruit. <u>S</u> stir until it is hot.
3. <u>T</u> the lights went out. <u>T</u> there was a thud. <u>S</u> someone screamed.

Finish the sentence.

4. When you toast bread it goes crispy.
5. When you run very fast your heart beats faster.
6. When you press the brakes on a bike it stops.

Cross out the verb. Write a new and more interesting verb.

7. He ~~went~~ through the brambles. scrambled
8. The monster ~~looked~~ at him. glared
9. The thunder ~~banged~~. boomed
10. Everyone ~~ran~~ away. scurried

> **PART C Focus**
> **1–3:** demarcating sentence boundaries
> **4–6:** forming sentences that show cause and effect
> **7–10:** choosing verbs for impact and precision

20

X DEFINITIVE ANSWER   X SAMPLE ANSWER

Section 2   Test 4

A WARM-UP

1 Write the sentence using different nouns.

The burglar stole a painting from the museum.

> PART A Focus
> **1:** nouns for precision.
> **2–5:** changing phonemes
> **6–9:** identifying synonyms
> **10:** common endings

The boy stole a bun from the baker.

Change one phoneme to make the word match the meaning.

2 peer   *poor*   means **not rich**

3 flat   *float*   means **to drift**

4 drown   *frown*   means **to scowl**

5 have   *heave*   means **to pull**

Underline the word that is a synonym of the word in **bold**.

6 **kind**   mean   cruel   <u>caring</u>   unkind

7 **strong**   weak   <u>mighty</u>   frail   feeble

8 **boring**   exciting   <u>dull</u>   thrilling

9 **ill**   untidy   <u>sick</u>   messy   well

10 The same syllable is missing from all these words. Write it in.

v a n <u>*ish*</u>   p u n <u>*ish*</u>   a s t o n <u>*ish*</u>

B WORD WORK

1 Add the same prefix to all three words.

un re de dis

<u>*re*</u> play   <u>*re*</u> fill   <u>*re*</u> write

2 How does it change the meaning?

The action is now being done again.

3 Write two more words with this prefix.

recycle   *replace*

> PART B Focus
> **1–3:** using prefixes
> **4–7:** verb synonyms; using a thesaurus
> **8–10:** common spelling errors

Write two verbs that mean the same as the verb in **bold**.

4 **laugh**   *chuckle*   *snigger*

5 **eat**   *gobble*   *munch*

6 **pull**   *heave*   *tug*

7 **weep**   *cry*   *sob*

Cross out the words that are wrongly spelt. Write the correct spelling.

8 Two ~~lorrys~~ were ~~driveing arownd.~~

lorries   *driving*   *around*

9 Some ~~childrun~~ were ~~droping~~ litter.

children   *dropping*

10 It is ~~allways coola~~ at ~~nite.~~

always   *cooler*   *night*

C SENTENCE WORK

Add **after**, **when** or **until**.

1 We watched TV <u>*until*</u> it was bedtime.

2 We watched TV <u>*after*</u> tea.

3 We watched TV <u>*when*</u> we came in.

> PART C Focus
> **1–3:** using connectives to show time relationships
> **4–5:** imperative verbs in instructions
> **6–9:** using capital letters
> **10:** past tense

4 Underline the verbs in these instructions.

<u>Add</u> the banana. <u>Beat</u> with a wooden spoon. <u>Empty</u> the yoghurt into a bowl. <u>Stir</u> well.

5 How are verbs used in instructions?   *They tell you what to do. They start the instruction.*

Write four reasons why capital letters have been used in this sentence.

Mr Jackson's class was silent. Then suddenly ... CRASH!

6 *For a title (Mr).*

7 *For a person's name (Jackson).*

8 *At the start of a sentence (Then).*

9 *For emphasis, to show a loud noise (CRASH).*

10 Write this sentence in the past tense.   **He knows it is late.**   *He knew it was late.*

Section 2   Test 5

A WARM-UP

Change the underlined words.

1 After they paddled in the sea,
Nathan and Sophie made a sandcastle.

   Lorna and Will had an ice cream.

2 When Marik saw the funfair,
When Sultan heard the roar, he began
to run.

These words and suffixes are mixed up.
Write them correctly.

properful **speech**ly **bead**less **wish**y

3 properly   5 speechless

4 beady   6 wishful

Add the missing vowel phoneme.

ea ee ie oa

*Clue: used in place of **said***

7 scr <u>ea</u> m e d   9 gr <u>oa</u> n e d

8 scr <u>ee</u> c h e d   10 shr <u>ie</u> k e d

> **PART A Focus**
> 1–2: composing sentences with linked parts
> 3–6: adding suffixes
> 7–10: correct spelling of phonemes; words in place of **said**

B WORD WORK

1 What do the words have in common?
know write half lamb
   They all have a silent letter.

2 What is the letter that is hidden?
   ■new ■now ■neel ■nit   k

3 Add an **ed** ending.
   chuckle chuckled   **cry** cried
   giggle giggled   **sob** sobbed

Write the new words as pairs of synonyms.

4 chuckled   and giggled
5 sobbed   and cried

Write the meaning of the word in **bold**.

6 **disqualify** ban, stop from taking part
7 **revisit**   return or visit again
8 **predict**   guess what will happen

Sort the movement verbs.

**creep thrash crawl scramble
scuttle charge drift edge**

9 **slow**   creep, crawl, drift, edge
10 **fast** thrash, scramble, scuttle, charge

> **PART B Focus**
> 1–2: silent letters
> 3: adding ed
> 4–5: synonyms
> 6–8: word meanings
> 9–10: choosing verbs for clarity

C SENTENCE WORK

Add a word to join the sentences. Do not use **and**.

1 Jack climbed until he reached the top.
2 It was dark so he took a torch.
3 The kite took off when the wind blew.

Underline the adjectives.

4 There was once a <u>beautiful</u> princess who lived in a <u>sparkling</u> palace on top of a <u>high</u>, <u>misty</u> mountain.

5 A thistle is a <u>wild</u> plant with <u>purple</u> flowers and <u>prickly</u> leaves.

6 What is the purpose of adjectives?
   They give more information about the things or people described.

Add anything that is missing.

7 "Can I come?" said the little girl.
8 "I can help you," said the mouse.
9 "What are you doing?" said Jenny.
10 "You shall go to the ball," said the Prince.

> **PART C Focus**
> 1–3: using connectives to link parts of a sentence
> 4–6: understanding adjectives
> 7–10: writing dialogue; speech punctuation

X DEFINITIVE ANSWER   X SAMPLE ANSWER

Section 2 Test 6

A WARM-UP

1 Extend the sentence so that it says **where** the Prince ran.

The Prince ran _out of the palace._

2 Add more so that it says **where and why**.

The Prince ran _out of the palace to_ _look for the missing Princesses._

Write four compound words ending with **ball**.
Write them in alphabetical order.

3 _basketball_   **5** _netball_

4 _football_   **6** _volleyball_

Underline the word that is **not** a synonym.

7 **shine** gleam <u>fade</u> glint

8 **brave** bold daring <u>weak</u>

9 **quick** fast <u>fine</u> swift

> **PART A Focus**
> **1–2**: extending sentences
> **3–6**: compound words; alphabetical order
> **7–9**: synonyms
> **10**: high-frequency words

10 The same two-letter word fits into all these longer words. Write it in.

w <u>h e</u> r e   t <u>h e</u> r e   <u>h e</u> l p

B WORD WORK

1 Complete the word sum.

1 **baby** × 2 = _2 babies_

1 **child** × 2 = _2 children_

1 **mouse** × 2 = _2 mice_

1 **fox** × 2 = _2 foxes_

> **PART B Focus**
> **1**: plural spelling rules and irregular words
> **2–6**: adding suffixes; word meanings
> **7–10**: topic words (food); using a dictionary

2 Add **er** and **est**.

small	_smaller_	_smallest_
rich	_richer_	_richest_
pale	_paler_	_palest_

Use one of the words you have made.

3 The Moon is _smaller_ than the Sun.

4 He was the _richest_ man in the land.

5 Pink is a _paler_ colour than red.

6 The King was _richer_ than the beggar.

Add the missing vowels.

Clue: found in food

7 f i b r e   **9** v i t a m i n s

8 c a r b o h y d r a t e s   **10** s u g a r

C SENTENCE WORK

Cross out the verb. Choose and write a new one.

produces powers pumps

1 The heart ~~sends~~ blood round the body. _pumps_

2 Electricity ~~works~~ many machines. _powers_

3 The honeybee ~~makes~~ the honey we eat. _produces_

> **PART C Focus**
> **1–3**: technical verbs for precision and accuracy
> **4–6**: choosing adjectives for effect; commas in lists of adjectives
> **7–10**: sentences that link several pieces of information

Write three adjectives that describe the item in **bold**.

4 Try this fresh, _crusty,_ _delicious,_ _brown_ **bread**.

5 Try this _smooth,_ _soft,_ _creamy_ **ice-cream**.

6 Try this _fast,_ _sleek,_ _thrilling_ **sports car**.

Write the notes as one complete sentence.

7 **dragonfly – insect – lives near water** _A dragonfly is an insect that lives near water._

8 **windows – glass – light pass** _Windows are made from glass so light can pass through._

9 **windmill sails – turn – power** _The sails on a windmill turn to produce power._

10 **spider – web – food** _A spider builds a web to catch food._

A　WARM-UP

The beginnings and endings of these sentences are mixed up.

Some dogs	moves round the Sun.
Frogs	dig holes.
An artist	eat flies.
The Earth	paints pictures.

> **PART A Focus**
> **1–4:** making sense; grammatical agreement
> **5–8:** identifying/ understanding prefixes
> **9–10:** prefixes and suffixes

Write the sentences correctly.

1　Some dogs dig holes.
2　Frogs eat flies.
3　An artist paints pictures.
4　The Earth moves round the Sun.

Underline the odd one out.

5　untrue <u>uniform</u> unfair unlock unreal
6　disagree distrust disallow <u>dishes</u> disorder
7　repay reform recycle reread <u>really</u>
8　Give a reason for your choices.
　　The letters at the start are not a prefix.

Add a word to complete the longer word.

9　u n __help__ f u l
10　d i s __appear__ i n g

B　WORD WORK

Add the missing syllable.

Clue: buildings

1　h o s __pit__ a l
2　s u p __er__ m a r __ket__
3　f a c __tor__ y

> **PART B Focus**
> **1–3:** using syllables for spelling
> **4–8:** rules for adding y
> **9–10:** inferring meaning

4　Add the suffix **y** to make the word an adjective.

crunch	crunchy
luck	lucky
sun	sunny
stone	stony

Use one of these adjectives to complete the phrase.

5　sunny day　　7　lucky number
6　stony ground　　8　crunchy apple

Write the meaning of the word in **bold**.

9　The people were **alarmed** by the blaze.
　'alarmed' means　worried
10　The gates **prevent** him from entering.
　'prevent' means　stop

C　SENTENCE WORK

Underline the adjectives.

1　The surface of the moon is <u>dry</u> and <u>dusty</u>.
2　Mercury is a <u>small</u>, <u>hot</u>, <u>rocky</u> planet.
3　Saturn is a <u>large</u> planet with <u>bright</u> rings.
4　Why have these adjectives been used in this piece of factual writing?
　　They give information about the size and features of the planets.

> **PART C Focus**
> **1–4:** use of adjectives
> **5–7:** punctuating speech; question and exclamation marks
> **8–10:** sentences that explain and give reasons; using **because** and **so**

Add the correct punctuation.

5　"What shall we do?" asked the little girl.
6　"Who's been sitting in my chair?" said father bear.
7　"Help!" shouted Jack.

Finish the sentence by adding information that explains.

8　Don't stand behind a moving swing because it could knock you over.
9　Eat lots of fruit and vegetables because they contain vitamins.
10　We keep milk in a fridge so it stays fresh.

X DEFINITIVE ANSWER　　X SAMPLE ANSWER

Section 2 Test 8

A WARM-UP

1 Write a sentence using these words.

paint but ladder

I wanted to paint the house but I
could not find the ladder.

Add the missing letters.

er ir ur

Clue: kinds of movement

2 w h _ir_ l   **4** c _ur_ l

3 s q u _ir_ m   **5** j _er_ k

6 Finish the sentence by giving a reason.

The old man smiled _because he was_
pleased to see me.

Add three letters to complete the word.

7 _t_ _r_ _i_ c k l e

8 _c_ _i_ _r_ c l e

9 _c_ _a_ _n_ d l e

10 _t_ _u_ _m_ b l e

> **PART A Focus**
> **1:** constructing compound sentences
> **2–5:** alternative spellings of ur verbs
> **6:** constructing sentences that explain/give reasons; using connectives
> **7–10:** the **le** spelling pattern

B WORD WORK

Make an adjective from the word in **bold** and use it to complete the sentence.

1 A bear has **fur**. It is ___ _furry_ ___ .

2 The silver coin **shines**. It is ___ _shiny_ ___ .

3 The film was **fun**. It was ___ _funny_ ___ .

4 **Snow** is falling. It is ___ _snowy_ ___ .

5 All these words have the same spelling pattern.

know knew knife knock

What is the pattern?

Silent 'k' is followed by 'n'.

Write three more words with the same pattern.

6 _Knee_   **8** _Knot_

7 _Knit_

Write two antonyms (opposites) for the word in **bold**.

9 The Prince was **kind**.

unkind   _mean_

10 The shop was **neat**.

untidy   _messy_

> **PART B Focus**
> **1–4:** adding y (doubling the final consonant if appropriate)
> **5–8:** silent k words
> **9–10:** antonyms; choice of adjectives

C SENTENCE WORK

Cross out the nouns and write them as plurals. Write the new sentence so that it makes sense.

1 Waiting inside was a ~~woman~~ with a ~~baby~~ and a ~~schoolchild.~~

Waiting inside _were two women with babies and two schoolchildren._

2 The old ~~lady~~ had a bad ~~foot.~~ _The old ladies had bad feet._

Finish the sentence.

3 The party went well until _Mum dropped the cake._

4 As he made his wish, _there was a huge puff of smoke._

Add the full stops and capital letters.

5 a̲ plant is a living thing.i̲t has a stem, leaves and roots.m̲ost plants grow in the earth.

6 m̲arch is the third month.i̲t has 31 days.i̲t is named after the r̲oman god m̲ars.

7 i̲t was late.d̲ylan had not come home.b̲j̲ and b̲ella were waiting for him.

Cross out the verb. Write a new verb that fits the mood.

8 The angry dog ~~barked~~ at the stranger.   _growled_

9 The grumpy old man ~~talked~~ to himself.   _muttered_

10 He happily ~~went~~ down the road.   _skipped_

> **PART C Focus**
> **1–2:** forming plurals; grammatical agreement
> **3–4:** using connectives
> **5–7:** punctuating sentence boundaries; using capitals
> **8–10:** choosing verbs for impact

A   WARM-UP

1 Underline the word that is **not** an adjective.

smooth   rough   <u>rock</u>   hard   powdery

2 Why is it not an adjective?

Because it is not a describing word.

3 Add a suffix to make it an adjective.

rock + y = rocky

> **PART A Focus**
> **1–3:** use of adjectives; adding y
> **4–5:** sentence variation; verbs
> **6–9:** compound words
> **10:** high-frequency words

Change the verb to make a new sentence.

He smiled at the boy.

4 He glared at the boy.

5 He screamed at the boy.

Write four compound words that start with **under**.

6 under ground   **8** under pass

7 under water   **9** under wear

10 The same two-letter word fits into all these longer words. Write it in.

u p <u>on</u>   s e c <u>on</u> d   <u>on</u> e

B   WORD WORK

Add **er** and **est**.

1 **crazy**   crazier   craziest

2 **flat**   flatter   flattest

3 **kind**   kinder   kindest

4 **gentle**   gentler   gentlest

Write the meaning of the word in **bold**.

5 This paper is **absorbent**.

'absorbent' means able to soak up liquids

6 The glass is **transparent**.

'transparent' means see-through

7 The plastic is **opaque**.

'opaque' means not see-through

Cross out the words that are wrongly spelt.
Write the correct spellings.

8 ~~Sudenly~~ I ~~stopt~~.

Suddenly   stopped

9 It has a ~~grate nuty~~ taste.

great   nutty

> **PART B Focus**
> **1–4:** adding er and est
> **5–7:** technical adjectives (properties of materials)
> **8–10:** common spelling errors

10 Take ~~harf~~ a pear and two ~~hole cherrys~~.

half   whole   cherries

C   SENTENCE WORK

Use one of these words to replace the words in **bold**.   **cavity   molars   bacteria**

1 Your **big back teeth** are used to chew food.   molars

2 Brush your teeth or **germs** will grow.   bacteria

3 You may get a **hole** in your tooth.   cavity

4 Underline the adjectives.

The alien had an <u>enormous</u> head with <u>round</u>, <u>bulging</u> eyes. Its <u>tiny</u> body was covered in <u>red pointed</u> scales. It had a <u>short brownish</u> tail with a <u>green</u> tuft on the end.

Write each adjective beside the type of thing it describes.

5 **colour**   brownish   green   red

6 **size**   tiny   enormous   short

7 **shape**   bulging   round   pointed

Complete the sentence so that it says **when** the event happened.

8 After eating his main course,   Abdul had a slice of apple pie.

9 Many years later,   the farmer became rich.

10 The snow melted   as the sun began to shine.

> **PART C Focus**
> **1–3:** using precise technical nouns; topic words (teeth)
> **4–7:** understanding and classifying adjectives
> **8–10:** phrases showing time relationships

26   X DEFINITIVE ANSWER   X SAMPLE ANSWER

A   WARM-UP

1 Add the suffix **y** to make an adjective.

powder	powdery
gloss	glossy
dust	dusty
shine	shiny

PART A Focus
1–3: rules for adding y; synonyms
4–7: spelling common time connectives
8: using connectives
9–10: writing two linked sentences

Write the words as pairs of synonyms.

2 powdery   **and**   dusty

3 glossy   **and**   shiny

Add the missing vowels.   *Clue: time connectives*

4 b e f o r e

6 s i n c e

5 m e a n w h i l e

7 u n t i l

8 Write a sentence using these words.

mouse when cat

The mouse ran into its hole when it saw the cat.

Write the notes as two complete sentences.

chess – board game – 64 squares

9 Chess is a board game.

10 It is played on a board with 64 squares.

B   WORD WORK

1 Underline the silent letter.

k n e e   g n a t

c r u m b   w r i n k l e d

PART B Focus
1: silent letters
2–5: syllables
6–7: using the suffix **able**
8–10: synonyms for adjectives; using a thesaurus

Add the missing syllable.

2 d i f fer e n t

4 t o mor r o w

3 i n tell i g e n t

5 a n i mal

6 Add the same suffix to all the words.

ful ly able less

enjoy able   drink able   read able

Use two of the words in this sentence.

7 The book was readable and enjoyable.

Write three synonyms for the word in **bold**.

8 **pretty** attractive   beautiful   lovely

9 **sly** crafty   cunning   shifty

10 **scary** frightening   alarming   terrifying

C   SENTENCE WORK

Add the punctuation and capital letters.

PART C Focus
1–3: punctuating dialogue
4–6: writing instructions; using imperatives
7–10: using connectives to link ideas in sentences

1 "who wants an ice-cream?" asked melanie.

2 "me!" screamed bobbie and robbie.

3 "what flavour do you want? there is mint or vanilla," explained melanie.

Rewrite the sentence so it sounds like an instruction.

4 We had to beat the eggs with a fork.   Beat the eggs with a fork.

5 The milk and sugar were added to the eggs.   Add the milk and sugar to the eggs.

6 We baked it for 25 minutes.   Bake it for 25 minutes.

Continue the sentence in four different ways.

7 Martha had very little money so she lived in a tiny house.

8 Martha had very little money because the wizard had stolen it from her.

9 Martha had very little money until she found the magic purse.

10 Martha had very little money but she was always cheerful.

A   WARM-UP

Continue the sentence.

1 The ball bounced <u>over the wall</u>

<u>and into the pond.</u>

2 The boy slipped <u>through the gap</u>

<u>in the fence and hid in the grass.</u>

Make three words using these letters only.

> **PART A Focus**
> **1–2:** extending sentences
> **3–9:** visual spelling strategies
> **10:** vowel phonemes

e i d t

3 <u>t i d e</u>   *Clue: changes in the sea*

4 <u>d i e t</u>   *Clue: the food you eat*

5 <u>t i e d</u>   *Clue: made a knot*

Add a short word to complete the longer word.

6 t o <u>get</u> h e r   **8** s u d <u>den</u> l y

7 b <u>all</u> o o n   **9** f o l <u>low</u> i n g

10 Add the same phoneme to all the words.

or ea ear air

s <u>ear</u> ch   <u>ear</u> th   l <u>ear</u> n

B   WORD WORK

Complete the word sums.

1 **greed + y =** <u>greedy</u> **+ est =** <u>greediest</u>

2 **sun + y =** <u>sunny</u> **+ est =** <u>sunniest</u>

3 **skin + y =** <u>skinny</u> **+ est =** <u>skinniest</u>

4 **scare + y =** <u>scary</u> **+ est =** <u>scariest</u>

Write three nouns that name types of

5 **aircraft** <u>helicopter</u> <u>jet</u> <u>rocket</u>

6 **storm** <u>blizzard</u> <u>hurricane</u> <u>gale</u>

7 **bird** <u>eagle</u> <u>vulture</u> <u>sparrow</u>

Write the pairs of words with the same spelling pattern. Add another similar word.

> **PART B Focus**
> **1–4:** rules for adding y and est
> **5–7:** precise nouns; using a thesaurus
> **8–9:** common spelling patterns
> **10:** common spelling errors; adding suffixes

found would sound should

8 <u>found</u> , <u>sound</u> and <u>round</u>

9 <u>would</u> , <u>should</u> and <u>could</u>

10 Cross out the words that are wrongly spelt. Write the correct spellings.

~~Carefuly~~ slice the ~~strawberrys~~.

<u>Carefully</u>   <u>strawberries</u>

C   SENTENCE WORK

Add the missing words to the dialogue. It begins, **"When will we see the sea?" asked Jamie.**

1 <u>"Very soon,"</u> replied Dad.

2 <u>"The sea! The sea!"</u> shouted Jamie excitedly.

> **PART C Focus**
> **1–2:** writing dialogue; speech punctuation
> **3–5:** linking information within a sentence
> **6–10:** past tense; spelling regular and irregular verbs

Write the notes as one complete sentence.

3 **mole – small animal – soft fur – underground**

<u>The mole is a small animal with soft fur that lives mainly underground.</u>

4 **frog – smooth, moist**   **toad – dry, rough**

<u>A frog's skin is smooth and moist but a toad's feels dry and rough.</u>

5 **wheat → flour → bread** <u>Wheat is made into flour, and flour is used to make bread.</u>

Cross out the verbs in the present tense. Write them in the past tense.

6 I ~~visit~~ my dad and he ~~takes~~ me out.   <u>visited</u>   <u>took</u>

7 The farmer ~~runs~~ and ~~hides~~ behind a rock.   <u>ran</u>   <u>hid</u>

8 The wizard ~~sits~~ and ~~writes~~ in his book of spells.   <u>sat</u>   <u>wrote</u>

9 The Prince ~~stops~~ and ~~grabs~~ his sword.   <u>stopped</u>   <u>grabbed</u>

10 The girl ~~sees~~ the old lady but ~~says~~ nothing.   <u>saw</u>   <u>said</u>

X DEFINITIVE ANSWER   X SAMPLE ANSWER

Section 2 Test 12

A WARM-UP

Cross out the nouns. Write new nouns to make a new sentence.

1 ~~A bull~~ has ~~horns~~.
  An elephant   *tusks*

2 ~~Tom~~ was ~~an elf~~ who lived in a ~~wood~~.
  Ben   *a rabbit*   *burrow*

Underline the correct spelling.

3 runy   <u>runny</u>   runnie

4 <u>happiest</u>   happyest   happyist

5 riseing   rissing   <u>rising</u>

Add different prefixes to the word **cover** to make three new words.

6 *re* cover

7 *dis* cover

8 *un* cover

> PART A Focus
> 1–2: selecting nouns for sentence variation
> 3–5: using suffixes
> 6–8: adding prefixes
> 9–10: compound words

9 Look at the separate parts of these words. Underline the odd one out.

without   inside   something   <u>follow</u>   anyone

10 Give a reason for your choice.
  It is not a compound word.

B WORD WORK

1 Add the silent letter.

k n i f e   *w* r i t e

h a l *f*   a n s w *w* e r

> PART B Focus
> 1: silent letters
> 2–6: adding suffixes; using words with able
> 7–10: topic words (weather)

2 Add the suffix **able**.

enjoy *able*   value *able*

agree *able*   comfort *able*

Use the words in these phrases.

3 a *comfortable* armchair

4 an *enjoyable* day out

5 a *valuable* diamond ring

6 a pleasant and *agreeable* man

7 Add the vowels. **Clue: weather**

r *a* *i* n f a l l   d r *o* *u* g h t   t *o* r n a d *o*

Use the words in these sentences.

8 A *tornado* tore up the trees.

9 There has been little *rainfall*.

10 There may soon be a *drought*.

C SENTENCE WORK

1 Write two sentences for a story. Use one of these words in each sentence.   **frog river**
  The little frog hopped off through the grass. Soon he came to a river.

2 Write two sentences for a report. Use one of the same two words in each sentence.
  A frog is a small animal with long back legs. It often lives near a river.

Write the notes as two complete sentences.   **leopard – cat family   lives – Asia   forests – climbs trees**

3 *The leopard is a member of the cat family and is found in parts of Asia.*

4 *It lives in forests and climbs trees.*

Add adjectives.

5 The house was *old* and *deserted* with a *broken* door and *overgrown* garden.

6 The *mysterious* man had a *thin* face with *sly* eyes.

7 The sky was *dark* with *grey* clouds covering the *silvery* moon.

> PART C Focus
> 1–2: writing linked sentences; fiction and factual writing
> 3–4: using notes to write complete and linked sentences
> 5–7: choosing adjectives for impact
> 8–10: proofreading for punctuation

Add the capital letters and punctuation.

8 *O* our senses allow us to see, feel, taste, hear and smell things.

9 *I* "i must warn the *K* king," said *I* ivan.

10 "don't do it," shouted *M* maria.

Remind the pupil to complete Section 2 of the Progress chart on page 46 of the workbook.

X **DEFINITIVE ANSWER**   X **SAMPLE ANSWER**   **29**

Schofield & Sims English Skills 2

Section 2 Writing task assessment sheet: Dressed for the weather

Name		Class/Set	
Teacher's name		Date	

Sentence structure and punctuation

	Always/often	Sometimes	Never
Develops ideas using simple, compound and some complex sentences			
Uses conjunctions to develop ideas within a sentence (e.g., **because**, **so**, **if**)			
Sentences demarcated accurately			
Capital letters used for names, etc.			
Uses commas in lists			
Uses generalised present tense			
Maintains appropriate use of person			
Subject and verb agreement correct			

Composition and effect

Information is well organised (e.g., using headings, paragraphs, topic sentences)			
Writer's viewpoint is clear (e.g., using an informative, advisory tone)			
Ideas are developed and expanded on through series of linked sentences			
Precise word choices, with appropriate technical vocabulary (e.g., **temperature**)			
Appropriate adjectives used to add detail (e.g., **padded jacket**, **woollen scarf**)			

Spelling

Words with regular vowel phonemes spelt correctly			
Compound words or words with phonically regular syllables spelt correctly			
High- or medium-frequency words correct			
Words using prefixes and suffixes spelt correctly (e.g., **icy**, **sunnier**, **comfortable**)			
Verb endings (**ing** and **ed**) correct (e.g., **sunbathing**, **skating**, **running**)			
Spelling of plurals correct			

Writing task summary

Schofield & Sims English Skills 2

Section 2 Completed proofreading task: The lost treasure

Name	Class/Set
Teacher's name	Date

The stoney path twistid up into the mowntains. there was a fearfull rumbul far away
but clara new she had to folow the path. there was no terning back. She was glad
she had her map, sord and majic clowk with her.

Clara scrambuld up the steap path untill she was lost in the mists and clowds. suddunley
the path became flata and the mist cleered. clara fownd she was standin by the bigist
cave she had ever seen. She creeps up to the edje of the cave. And peers inside.

Just at that moment there was a mightey roer and a powerfull voyce. "Who dares come
to the cave of zog?" it cryed.

Proofreading task summary

Section 2 tasks summary

From: **English Skills 2 Answers** by Carol Matchett (ISBN 978 07217 1182 9). Copyright © Schofield & Sims Ltd, 2011. Published by Schofield & Sims Ltd,
Dogley Mill, Fenay Bridge, Huddersfield HD8 0NQ, UK (www.schofieldandsims.co.uk). **This page may be photocopied for use within your school or institution only.**

Section 3 Test 1

Add the missing syllable. *Clue: shapes*

1 p y _ra_ m i d
2 h e x _a_ g o n
3 r e c _tan_ g l e
4 t r i _an_ g l e

Finish the sentence.

5 The monster ate _three cars for_ _breakfast._

6 He lived in a cave _high up in_ _the mountains._

7 He roared _when people threw_ _things at him._

8 The monster was sad _because_ _he had no friends._

Sort the words into two sets of synonyms.

sturdy weak powerful feeble
powerless frail burly strong

PART A Focus
1–4: syllables; topic words (shapes) **5–8:** extending sentences **9–10:** synonyms

9 _weak, feeble, powerless, frail_
10 _strong, powerful, burly, sturdy_

1 What spelling pattern do these words share?

write wreck wrinkle wrong

Silent 'w' comes before 'r'.

Write four more words with same pattern.

2 _wrap_
3 _wretch_
4 _wriggle_
5 _wrist_

Add a suffix to each word. Write it in one of the sentences.

mouth amaze

PART B Focus
1–5: the spelling pattern wr; using a dictionary **6–7:** using suffixes **8–10:** synonyms; using a thesaurus

6 He tasted a _mouthful_ .
7 He looked round in _amazement_ .

Write three synonyms of the word in **bold**.

8 The man wore **nice** clothes.
   smart _expensive_ _elegant_

9 The burglar **went** up the path.
   crept _sneaked_ _tiptoed_

10 There was a **sound** of machinery.
   hum _buzz_ _clank_

Cross out a verb or verb phrase and use one of these instead. **hibernate migrate survive**

1 Many animals find it hard to ~~live~~ in winter. _survive_
2 Some of them ~~go to sleep.~~ _hibernate_
3 Some birds ~~fly away.~~ _migrate_
4 Why are the new verbs better choices? _They are the correct scientific words._

Write the sentence as a line of dialogue.

5 Ben asked his mum for help. _"Mum, can you help me?" asked Ben._
6 Josh shouted hello to Ravi. _"Hello, Ravi!" shouted Josh._
7 Katie asked the time. _"What time is it?" asked Katie._

8 Add the capital letters and full stops.

   _E_   _T_   _H_
   emily turned. there was a wolf. he was standing right behind her.

PART C Focus
1–4: precise or technical verbs **5–7:** punctuating dialogue **8:** punctuating sentence boundaries **9–10:** combining information within sentences; writing linked sentences

9 Rewrite the sentences as one complete sentence.
   Emily turned and saw a wolf standing right behind her.

10 Write another sentence that says what happened next.
   She screamed so loudly that the wolf ran away.

X DEFINITIVE ANSWER   X SAMPLE ANSWER

Section 3   Test 2

A   WARM-UP

1 Add the missing silent letters.

c a s <u>t</u> l e   s <u>w</u> o r d   r <u>h</u> y m e

Make four words using these words and suffixes only.

cheer quiet ful ness er y

2	cheerful	**4**	cheery
3	quietness	**5**	quieter

The beginnings and endings of these sentences are mixed up.

Fish work in schools.
Teachers bark loudly.
Some dogs have humps.
Camels live in water.

PART A Focus
1: silent letters
2–5: using suffixes
6–9: making sense
10: high-frequency words

Write the sentences correctly.

6 Fish live in water.
7 Teachers work in schools.
8 Some dogs bark loudly.
9 Camels have humps.

10 Make two words using these letters only.

a s w   <u>was</u> and <u>saw</u>

B   WORD WORK

1 What is missing from these words?

dont isnt Ive weve

Apostrophes to show where letters are missing.

Write the shortened forms correctly.

PART B Focus
1–5: apostrophes in shortened forms
6–8: word meanings; using a dictionary
9–10: synonyms for common adjectives

2	don't	**4**	I've
3	isn't	**5**	we've

Write a synonym of the word in **bold**.

6	He was a **troublesome** boy.	difficult
7	That's **precisely** what I meant.	exactly
8	He was **dumbfounded**.	amazed

Sort the words into two groups.

caring thoughtful heartless spiteful
unfeeling ruthless considerate unselfish

9	**kind**	caring, thoughtful, considerate, unselfish
10	**cruel**	heartless, spiteful, unfeeling, ruthless

C   SENTENCE WORK

Complete the sentence. Add commas where they are needed.

1 Mrs Gill shut the front door, locked it, put the key in her bag and <u>climbed into her car.</u>

2 Tom stamped his feet, flung down his bag, screwed up his face and <u>screamed loudly.</u>

3 The magician stood up, waved his wand, said the magic words and <u>disappeared.</u>

Use one of these words to complete the sentence.   **if since though**

PART C Focus
1–3: using commas in a list of actions; completing sentences appropriately
4–6: connectives in sentences
7–10: choosing words for precision and clarity

4 I like playing football <u>though</u> I'm not that good at it.

5 We have lived here <u>since</u> I was five.

6 I know I will do it <u>if</u> I keep trying.

Read this.   **The man went out of the building. The wind blew.**

How could you make the sentences more interesting? Explain two ways.

7 By using more interesting verbs.   **8** By using interesting adjectives.

Improve the sentence.

9 The man went out.   The King hurried from his frozen castle.

10 The wind blew.   The icy north wind raged.

X **DEFINITIVE ANSWER**   X **SAMPLE ANSWER**   **33**

Section 3 Test 3

A WARM-UP

1 Write a sentence using these nouns.

giant flower garden

The giant picked a flower in
the garden.

Add the missing letters.

Clue: parts of your hand

> **PART A Focus**
> **1:** forming a longer sentence
> **2–5:** words with silent letters
> **6–9:** alternative spelling of vowel phoneme
> **10:** extending a simple sentence

2 w r _i_ _s_ t   **4** k n _u_ _c_ _k_ l _e_

3 t h _u_ _m_ _b_

5 What do the words have in common?

They all have a silent letter.

Add the missing letters.

er ear ir ur

6 t h _ir_ s t y   **8** m i s h _ear_ d

7 h _ur_ t f u l   **9** a f t _er_

Add more information about the event.

10 Ruby remembered _what the stranger_
had told her.

B WORD WORK

Add these suffixes to the word **happy**.

ness er est ly

1 happiness   **3** happiest

2 happier   **4** happily

Add verb endings.

5 We went swim _ming_ , sunbathe _ing_
and paddle _ing_ .

6 They came run _ning_ , skid _ding_ and
hurtle _ing_ into the playground.

7 Write a synonym of the word in **bold**.

gruffly   grumpily

immensely   hugely

gleefully   happily

> **PART B Focus**
> **1–4:** adding suffixes to words ending with y
> **5–6:** rules for adding ing
> **7–10:** synonyms; the suffix ly; using a thesaurus

Use the synonyms in these sentences.

8 The little boy laughed _happily_ .

9 The task was _hugely_ difficult.

10 "Why?" he asked _grumpily_ .

C SENTENCE WORK

Add the punctuation and capital letters.

1 mr marshall found a dusty old picture in his house in lexton somerset

2 was it worth anything the answer is yes

3 mr marshall told our reporter, I was most surprised to hear it was valuable.

Underline the verbs.

4 The man's eyes <u>flashed</u> as he <u>glared</u> at Simon.   **5** He <u>stomped</u> around, <u>muttering</u> to himself.

6 What do these verbs tell us about the character?   That he was angry

Write the sentences with different verbs to change the mood of the character.

7 The man's eyes twinkled as he smiled at Simon.

8 He danced around, singing to himself.

Rewrite the information in one sentence.

> **PART C Focus**
> **1–3:** punctuating sentences
> **4–8:** choosing verbs for effect
> **9–10:** combining information within a sentence

9 Stir the mixture. Use a wooden spoon. Stop when it is golden brown.

Stir the mixture with a wooden spoon until it is golden brown.

10 A bat is a small animal. It looks like a mouse. It has wings.

A bat is a small animal that looks rather like a mouse but has wings.

34   X DEFINITIVE ANSWER   X SAMPLE ANSWER

Section 3 Test 4

A WARM-UP

These words and suffixes are mixed up.
Write them correctly.

goodless hairful regretness

1	*goodness*	3	*regretful*
2	*hairless*		

PART A Focus
1–3: suffixes
4–5: using connectives within sentences
6–8: choosing correct spelling of vowel phoneme
9–10: choosing verbs for effect

Finish the sentence.

4 **While she waited,** *it began to get dark.*

5 **As darkness fell,** *it grew cooler.*

Add the missing letters.

oar our ar

6 p *our* e d   8 s w *ar* m e d

7 s *oar* e d

Change the verbs.

9 **They** ~~strolled~~ **down the road,**
~~laughing~~ **and** ~~joking.~~

   raced   *shouting*   *screaming*

10 **Trees** ~~whispered~~ **and** ~~waved~~ **in the wind.**

   groaned   *creaked*

B WORD WORK

Write the words in their shortened form.

1	**does not**	*doesn't*
2	**she has**	*she's*
3	**I would**	*I'd*
4	**will not**	*won't*

PART B Focus
1–4: apostrophes in shortened forms
5: prefixes
6–8: defining words; using a dictionary
9–10: sorting topic words; synonyms for colours

5 Underline the prefix.

   <u>dis</u>connect   <u>mis</u>place   <u>re</u>arrange

Write a definition (the meaning).

6 'disconnect' means *cut off or unplug*

7 'misplace' means *lose*

8 'rearrange' means *organise differently*

Sort the words into two groups.

red purple lavender mauve scarlet
burgundy cherry violet lilac crimson

9 *red, crimson, scarlet, burgundy, cherry*

10 *purple, violet, lilac, lavender, mauve*

C SENTENCE WORK

Underline the pronouns.

1 **My sister was waiting so <u>I</u> picked up <u>my</u> bag and <u>we</u> left.**

2 **<u>We</u> will meet <u>you</u> at the end of <u>your</u> road with <u>our</u> bikes.**

3 **<u>She</u> was so late that <u>they</u> grew restless waiting for <u>her</u>.**

4 **<u>He</u> invented <u>it</u> in <u>his</u> workshop.**

PART C Focus
1–4: identifying pronouns
5–7: use of adjectives
8–10: extending sentences appropriately using connectives

Cross out any unnecessary adjectives.

5 **They warmed their icy hands by the** ~~boiling hot~~ **fire.**

6 **He lived in a** ~~great big,~~ **huge,** ~~enormous~~ **mansion.**

7 Why are the extra adjectives not needed?

Because they just say the same thing/they don't add anything new to the description.

Continue the sentence about a story you have read.

8 **I have chosen this story because** *I read it recently.*

9 **You will enjoy this story if** *you like adventure stories.*

10 **I liked the story though** *I guessed the ending.*

Section 3　Test 5

A　WARM-UP

Add a short word to complete the longer word.

1 in <u>for</u> m a t i o n　**3** c h a r <u>act</u> e r

2 i n t e <u>rest</u> i n g　**4** c o n <u>tin</u> u e

5 Use these words to make five compound words.

in　out　ways　with　side

<u>inside, within, outside, without, sideways</u>

Add a word to the sentence.

6 The hare was <u>faster</u> than the tortoise.

7 A book is <u>heavier</u> than a feather.

8 A mango is <u>bigger</u> than an apple.

9 What do all the words have in common?

<u>They all end with the suffix 'er'.</u>

10 Write a sentence using these verbs.

snarled　wriggled

<u>The giant snarled as Jack</u>

<u>wriggled to get free.</u>

> **PART A Focus**
> **1–4:** visual spelling strategies
> **5:** compound words
> **6–9:** comparatives; adding er
> **10:** forming a sentence

B　WORD WORK

Add a suffix to the word in **bold** so that it matches the definition.

1 **cheer** <u>less</u>　sad and gloomy

2 **harm** <u>ful</u>　dangerous

3 **child** <u>ish</u>　silly

4 **near** <u>ly</u>　almost

> **PART B Focus**
> **1–4:** suffixes; word meanings
> **5–7:** spelling rules for plurals
> **8–10:** technical words; using a dictionary to check meaning

Change the nouns into plurals.

5 The ~~leaf~~ fluttered on the ~~branch~~.

<u>leaves</u>　　<u>branches</u>

6 We took the ~~loaf~~ off the ~~shelf~~.

<u>loaves</u>　　<u>shelves</u>

7 The furry ~~bunny~~ rode in the ~~buggy~~.

<u>bunnies</u>　　<u>buggies</u>

Use one of these words in the sentence.

structure　inflatable　reclaimed

8 This airbed is <u>inflatable</u> .

9 We built a tall <u>structure</u> .

10 We used <u>reclaimed</u> materials.

C　SENTENCE WORK

Add punctuation to the dialogue.

1 "Have you remembered the box?" asked Julia.

2 "We are nearly there," said Max.

3 "That's it!" shouted Nick. "Let's go!"

4 "Be careful. It's very icy," warned Joe.

> **PART C Focus**
> **1–4:** punctuating dialogue
> **5–7:** time connectives
> **8–10:** choosing words for precision and clarity

Use one of these connectives to replace **then**.

After that,　**Suddenly**,　**Eventually**

5 It was a long journey. ~~Then~~ <u>Eventually</u> they arrived.

6 We watched the match. ~~Then~~ <u>After that</u> we had tea.

7 They fell asleep. ~~Then~~ <u>Suddenly</u> the phone rang.

Improve the report by changing the words in **bold**. Write the sentence with the new words in place.

8 We **got** the rainwater in the **pot**.　<u>We collected the rainwater in the measuring jug.</u>

9 Then we can **see how much rain there is**.　<u>Then we can measure the rainfall.</u>

10 We **put** the **numbers** on a **paper**.　<u>We record the measurements on a chart.</u>

　X DEFINITIVE ANSWER　X SAMPLE ANSWER

Section 3   Test 6

A WARM-UP

Write four words ending with **ness**.

1 _happiness_   3 _Kindness_

2 _gentleness_   4 _gladness_

5 Add the correct double letters.

h o _bb_ l e

g i _gg_ l e

g u _zz_ l e

PART A Focus
1–4: the suffix ness
5: double letters followed by le
6–10: using connectives; ending sentences appropriately

Continue the sentence.

6 King Crumble was happy if _everyone obeyed him._

7 King Crumble was happy because _he had a loving family._

8 King Crumble was happy until _King Grumble came to stay._

9 King Crumble was happy so _he gave presents to his friends._

10 King Crumble was happy though _he was no longer rich._

B WORD WORK

Write the correct spelling.

1 **crum**   _crumb_

2 **rino**   _rhino_

3 **rubarb**   _rhubarb_

PART B Focus
1–4: silent letters
5–7: proofreading for common spelling errors
8–10: synonyms; choosing words for impact

4 Why were the spellings wrong?
   The silent letter was missing.

Write the sentence correctly.

5 ~~Its the hotist day ov the yeer!~~
   It's the hottest day of the year!

6 ~~Ive seen a family of foxis~~
   I've seen a family of foxes.

7 ~~He droppt the rapper in the rode.~~
   He dropped the wrapper in the road.

Write an adjective that is stronger than the word in **bold**.

8 It was a **horrible** sight.   _hideous_

9 The book was **interesting**.   _fascinating_

10 She was **surprised**.   _astonished_

C SENTENCE WORK

Add a comma.

1 Food helps us to grow, gives us energy and keeps us healthy.

PART C Focus
1–3: commas in lists of phrases
4–6: using pronouns
7–10: time connectives in different types of text

Add three phrases to complete the sentence.

2 An elephant uses its trunk to _hold things, reach food and drink water._

3 Seeds are dispersed by _the wind, by animals and by water._

Add pronouns.

4 Charles Dickens was a writer. _He_ wrote many novels. _They_ were very popular.

5 Ducks are birds that swim. _They_ have webbed feet. Many of _them_ feed in fresh water.

6 Milk comes from cows. _It_ is an important food. _It_ gives _us_ protein and minerals.

Choose two connectives to use in instructions and two to use in a story.

Next, At that moment, Continue to, But meanwhile

7 **instructions** _Next, Continue to_

8 **story** _At that moment, But meanwhile_

Continue the sentence.

9 The shadowy figure disappeared. Minutes later _it reappeared, carrying something._

10 Sieve the flour into the bowl. Next _add the sugar._

Section 3 Test 7

A WARM-UP

Write an antonym.

1 inflate   *deflate*

2 input   *output*

3 equal   *unequal*

> **PART A Focus**
> **1–3:** antonyms; prefixes
> **4–5:** spelling plurals
> **6–7:** extending sentences
> **8–10:** onomatopoeia; vowel phonemes

Write each noun as a plural.

4 puppy   kitten   mouse

   puppies   *kittens*   *mice*

5 prince   princess   wolf

   princes   *princesses*   *wolves*

Add more information about the event.

6 He waited outside the bank *for the*
   robbers to appear.

7 He opened the chest carefully *so no-one*
   would hear.

Add the missing vowel phoneme.

Clue: they sound like a sound

8 c r _ea_ k   10 w h _oo_ s h

9 b l _ee_ p

B WORD WORK

1 Complete the verb sum.

> **PART B Focus**
> **1–2:** adding **ed** to verbs ending with y
> **3–6:** word definitions; use of dictionary
> **7–10:** adding prefixes

scurry + ed = *scurried*

display + ed = *displayed*

replay + ed = *replayed*

reply + ed = *replied*

2 What spelling rule did you use?

If a word ends 'consonant y',
change the 'y' to an 'i' and add 'ed'.

Write the verb beside the correct definition.

construct examine recommend magnify

3 *examine*   look at closely

4 *magnify*   enlarge

5 *construct*   build

6 *recommend*   suggest

Add the same prefix to all three words.

7 *anti* freeze   *anti* septic   *anti* clockwise

8 *mis* read   *mis* behave   *mis* understand

9 *non* -stick   *non* -fiction   *non* sense

10 *ex* claim   *ex* plain   *ex* change

C SENTENCE WORK

Add the missing punctuation and capital letters.

> **PART C Focus**
> **1–3:** checking punctuation; writing letters
> **4–7:** using adjectives for clarity; avoiding overuse or inappropriate use of adjectives
> **8–10:** grammatical agreement

1 **D**ear **M**rs **J**enkins,
   You are a winner! **Y**ou have won first prize in our competition.

2 **H**i **J**oss,
   We will meet you and **A**ndy at **P**enley station on **S**aturday. **S**ee you then.

3 **D**ear **M**r **C**larke,
   I enjoyed greatly your book **C**old **T**imes. **Y**ou are my favourite author.

Choose the one adjective that works best and cross out the others.

4 The ~~cute~~ kiwi is a ~~brown~~ flightless bird.   5 The ~~scary stripy~~ tiger is a powerful creature.

How did you choose the adjectives to cross out? Give two reasons.

6 *Words like 'cute' and 'scary' don't sound correct in factual writing.*

7 *Some adjectives didn't add any information (e.g. all tigers are stripy).*

Cross out the words that do not sound right. Write the correct words.

8 "I ~~is~~ hungry," said the alien. "What ~~does~~ you eat on ~~you~~ planet?"   *am*   *do*   *your*

9 "I ~~likes~~ it here. Everyone ~~are~~ very ~~friendy~~ to ~~my~~."   *like*   *is*   *friendly*   *me*

10 "I ~~thinks~~ there ~~is~~ lots more ~~peoples~~ for ~~I~~ to meet."   *think*   *are*   *people*   *me*

X DEFINITIVE ANSWER   X SAMPLE ANSWER

A WARM-UP

Write a sentence using these words.

1 moon dog street *The dog sat in the street howling at the moon.*

2 water park kite *The kite soared above the park then landed in the water.*

Write three words that rhyme with the word in **bold**.

3	**chair**	*care*	*bear*	*stair*
4	**four**	*more*	*floor*	*paw*
5	**turn**	*burn*	*fern*	*earn*

Sort the connectives into two groups.

> **PART A Focus**
> **1–2:** forming sentences
> **3–5:** long vowel phonemes
> **6–7:** time connectives
> **8–10:** adding er and est

Just then, Finally, Later,

At once, Eventually, Suddenly

6 In the end *Finally, Later, Eventually*

7 Right then *Suddenly, Just then, At once*

Complete the word chain.

cold colder coldest

8	hot	*hotter*	*hottest*
9	fast	*faster*	*fastest*
10	heavy	*heavier*	*heaviest*

B WORD WORK

Write a definition of the word in **bold**.

1 We went on a **train**.

train: *a vehicle that runs on rails*

2 We **train** daily for the race.

train: *to exercise, practise*

> **PART B Focus**
> **1–5:** homonyms; using context to work out meaning
> **6–10:** understanding and using apostrophes

3 She put the **ring** on her finger.

ring: *a piece of jewellery*

4 A bell began to **ring**.

ring: *to make a clear, loud sound*

5 What do you notice about the words **train** and **ring**?

They have more than one meaning.

Write the word with the apostrophe in the correct place. Then write the full form.

6	**shell'**	*she'll*	*she will*
7	**well'**	*we'll*	*we will*
8	**were'**	*we're*	*we are*
9	**shed'**	*she'd*	*she would (or she had)*
10	**youd**	*you'd*	*you would (or you had)*

C SENTENCE WORK

Write these lines so that the **said** part is in the middle of the dialogue, not at the end.

> **PART C Focus**
> **1–3:** punctuating dialogue
> **4–6:** verbs chosen for effect
> **7–10:** using pronouns

1 "What are you doing here? This is private land," said the man.

"What are you doing here?" said the man. "This is private land."

2 "I am Zoll. I come from the planet Kroll," said the alien.

"I am Zoll," said the alien. "I come from the planet Kroll."

3 "Sophie, I want to speak to you," said Mum.

"Sophie," said Mum. "I want to speak to you."

Write a word to use instead of **said**. Make the character sound angry.

4 *demanded* the man

5 *growled* the alien

6 *shouted* Mum

Read the sentence. Pretend you are Oscar. Write the sentence in the first person.

7 Oscar sold his mother's best cooking pot. *I sold my mother's best cooking pot.*

8 It belonged to Oscar's mother not to him. *It belonged to my mother not to me.*

9 Should Oscar give the money to his mother? *Should I give the money to my mother?*

10 Or should he keep it for himself? *Or should I keep it for myself?*

A WARM-UP

Change the nouns so the sentence gives a different picture.

1 A ~~man~~ stood by the ~~door~~ holding a ~~briefcase~~.

<u>wizard</u>   <u>cave</u>   <u>broomstick</u>

2 The ~~fox~~ followed the ~~chicken~~ into the ~~farmyard~~.

<u>policeman</u>   <u>thief</u>   <u>hideout</u>

3 The ~~baker~~ put the ~~cake~~ in the ~~oven~~.

<u>pirate</u>   <u>map</u>   <u>chest</u>

Add **ee** and/or **ea** to complete the word.

4 s_ea_w_ee_d

6 sw_ee_th_ea_rt

5 ch_ee_rl_ea_der

7 h_ea_dg_ea_r

Underline the two words in each list that have more than one meaning.

8 ice <u>spot</u> day chin <u>bat</u>

9 <u>light</u> ear <u>wave</u> flour big

10 <u>rose</u> frog <u>leaves</u> grass bud

> **PART A Focus**
> **1–3:** choice of nouns; sentence variation
> **4–7:** alternative vowel phonemes
> **8–10:** homonyms

B WORD WORK

Write a more formal synonym for the word in **bold**.

1 **Stick** it to the wall.   <u>attach</u>

2 It was a **nice** view.   <u>spectacular</u>

3 Underline the prefix.

<u>de</u>mist   <u>de</u>bug   <u>de</u>frost

4 What does the prefix mean?

<u>to do the opposite or reverse</u>

> **PART B Focus**
> **1–2:** synonyms
> **3–4:** the prefix **de**
> **5–9:** plural spelling of words ending in y
> **10:** syllables; word meanings

Make the word into a plural.

5 **lady** <u>ladies</u>   **7** **hobby** <u>hobbies</u>

6 **diary** <u>diaries</u>   **8** **baby** <u>babies</u>

9 What rule did you use to help you?

<u>If a word ends 'consonant y',</u>

<u>change the 'y' to an 'i' and add 'es'.</u>

10 Add the missing syllables.

Clue: finding and bringing together

dis_cov_ering   col_lect_ing

C SENTENCE WORK

Improve the sentence by changing the words in **bold**.

1 We hope to **do up** the school library.   <u>refit</u>

2 Mrs Hawkins will **give** the prize.   <u>present</u>

3 We hope to **make** some money.   <u>raise</u>

4 Why are your words better than the words in **bold**?   <u>They sound more formal.</u>

> **PART C Focus**
> **1–4:** choosing verbs for clarity
> **5–6:** use of exclamation marks
> **7–10:** subordination; using connectives

5 Add two full stops and two exclamation marks.

SLAM! Everyone stood very still. Yes, it was a magic carpet! No-one moved for a long time.

6 Why did you decide to use exclamation marks where you did?

<u>To show that what happened made a loud noise or was surprising or exciting.</u>

7 Write the sentence again so that it starts with the word **while**.

The snow began to fall while everyone slept.   <u>While everyone slept, the snow began to fall.</u>

Finish the sentence.

8 As the snow fell on the houses,   <u>the town turned into a magical place.</u>

9 When the people awoke,   <u>they saw the smooth, unmarked snow.</u>

10 Because it was so cold,   <u>the water had frozen.</u>

X DEFINITIVE ANSWER   X SAMPLE ANSWER

A   WARM-UP

Finish the second sentence.

1 Jack searched for the gold. Before long,

he found something.

2 Jack searched for the gold. Meanwhile,

Jill tried to solve the riddle.

Write two synonyms for the word in **bold**.

3 **shake**   _quiver_   _tremble_

4 **hungry**   _starving_   _famished_

5 **creep**   _sneak_   _tiptoe_

> **PART A Focus**
> **1–2:** linked sentences; time connectives
> **3–5:** synonyms; word choice
> **6–9:** synonyms; vowel phonemes
> **10:** forming sentences

Add the missing phoneme.

Clue: *light*

6 g l _ea_ m

8 g l _ow_

7 s p _ar_ k l e

9 b _ea_ m

10 Write a sentence using these words.

cat bowl suitcase

The cat found its bowl in a suitcase.

B   WORD WORK

Write a definition of the word in **bold**.

1 They began to **row** down the river.

to move a boat using oars

2 We put out a **row** of chairs.

a line

3 There was a terrible **row** afterwards.

a quarrel

What do you notice about the word **row**?

4 _it has more than one meaning_

5 _it can be said in two different ways_

These words and suffixes are mixed up.
Write them correctly.

bagable relyful painy

6 _baggy_

8 _reliable_

7 _painful_

> **PART B Focus**
> **1–5:** homonyms; using context to work out meaning
> **6–8:** adding suffixes; spelling rules
> **9–10:** checking spelling

Correct the spelling.

9 Peepul shud laff moore.

People should laugh more.

10 The teem playd betta in the furst harf.

The team played better in the first half.

C   SENTENCE WORK

Continue the sentence.

1 Plants will not grow unless _they have water._

2 Houseplants do not grow outside because _it is too cold._

3 Protect your outdoor plants if _there is a frost._

4 Underline the verbs.

The van <u>raced</u> down the high street, <u>swerving</u> from one side to the other.

5 Why were these verbs chosen?   _to make the sentence exciting_

Cross out the verbs. Write new verbs that make the animal sound angry.

6 The animal ~~went~~ down the street, ~~looking~~ around him.   _thundered_   _glaring_

7 The animal ~~hopped~~ from the branch and ~~squeaked~~ at the birds.   _leapt_   _shrieked_

Add the capital letters and punctuation to the extract from a dialogue.

8 "Climb up here," said the snake. "It is quite safe."

9 "What's that?" asked the farmer. "Is it gold?"

10 "Oh thank you," sobbed the girl.

> **PART C Focus**
> **1–3:** using connectives to explain or introduce a reason
> **4–7:** choosing verbs for impact
> **8–10:** punctuating dialogue

A WARM-UP

Underline the word that is **not** a real word.

1 careless tuneless <u>tiredless</u> homeless

2 readable bendable breakable <u>dashable</u>

3 prouder nearer <u>painer</u> driver

Continue the sentence so that it explains why.

4 She was excited *at the thought of* *a month at the seaside.*

5 He dashed out of the house *as the fire began to spread.*

6 The Moon is different from the Earth *because it has no water.*

Add a short word to complete the longer word.

7 *of* t e n

8 a l *on* g

9 s o *me* t i m e s

10 b e c a *us* e

PART A Focus
1–3: suffixes
4–6: continuing sentences
7–10: high-frequency words; visual spelling skills

B WORD WORK

1 Write the prefix beside its definition.

re pre anti

re   again

anti   against

pre   before

PART B Focus
1–4: prefixes
5–7: homonyms
8–10: antonyms

Write two words starting with the prefix.

2 **re**   *reform*   *replace*

3 **pre**   *prefix*   *predict*

4 **anti**   *anticlockwise*   *antibiotic*

Write two different definitions.

5 **gum**   *where your teeth fit* / *something people chew*

6 **fit**   *healthy and strong* / *to be the correct shape and size*

7 **pop**   *to burst suddenly* / *a drink*

Complete the pairs of antonyms.

8 cheap and *expensive*

9 boring and *interesting*

10 awful and *wonderful*

C SENTENCE WORK

Add a connective to link the two ideas.

1 "I did it *because* I thought you would be pleased."

2 "We can try *but* I'm not very hopeful."

3 "Let's tidy up *while* Mum is out."

PART C Focus
1–3: connectives within sentences
4–6: using punctuation to clarify meaning
7–10: using adjectives for clarity

Add the capital letters and punctuation.

4 Buzzz! What was that? It was too loud to be a fly. What could it be?

5 They shouted. No-one came. They shouted again but still no-one came.

6 It was a great big elephant! An elephant in their front garden!

Write the sentence again using at least three adjectives.

7 The woman carried a box with a lid.
The old woman carried a tiny wooden box with a gold lid.

8 The castle was made of bricks and had five turrets.
The sparkling castle was made of silver bricks and had five tall turrets.

9 He wore a hat and a cloak made of feathers.
He wore a floppy hat and a flowing cloak made of multicoloured feathers.

10 How do the adjectives improve the sentences? *They help to create a clearer picture.*

X DEFINITIVE ANSWER   X SAMPLE ANSWER

A WARM-UP

Finish the sentence.

1. Matt did not listen because _he was in a hurry._

2. Matt did not listen when _his father warned him not to go._

3. Matt did not listen until _it was too late._

Use the same word to complete both phrases.

4. wrist _watch_   _watch_ dog

5. traffic _jam_   toast and _jam_

6. _flat_ for sale   _flat_ as a pancake

7. The same letters are missing from all these words. Write them in.

t _igh_ t l y   f r _igh_ t e n

m _igh_ t y   h _igh_ l _igh_ t

Add the missing syllables.

8. mis _for_ _tune_   bad luck

9. bell _ow_ _ing_   shouting

10. thou _sand_   a large number

PART A Focus
1–3: using connectives
4–6: homonyms
7: the spelling pattern igh
8–10: syllables

B WORD WORK

Use the prefixes and suffixes to make four new words from the word **fold**.

un re er able

1. _unfold_   3. _refold_

2. _folder_   4. _foldable_

Use two of the words you have made.

5. This box is _foldable_ .

6. I'll fold it and then _refold_ it.

Write a definition of the word in **bold**.

7. This box is **recyclable**.
   can be recycled or used again

8. The door is **unhinged**.
   has come off its hinges

PART B Focus
1–6: using prefixes and suffixes
7–8: deducing meaning from context and word parts
9–10: common spelling errors

Underline the words that are wrongly spelt. Write the correct spellings.

9. I tryed that onse but neva agayn.
   tried   _once_   _never_   _again_

10. The leefs swerl arownd the gardin.
    leaves   _swirl_   _around_   _garden_

C SENTENCE WORK

Complete the sentence.

1. As _the ship came closer_ , Mack began to smile.

2. If _they did not hurry_ , it would be too late.

3. Before _they could sit down_ , the classroom door flew open.

4. When _he arrived_ , he found Marie already waiting.

PART C Focus
1–4: adding clauses; using connectives
5–7: choosing words for precision
8–10: checking punctuation and grammar

Rewrite the sentence so that it is clearer and more interesting.

5. The children went to see the thing. _The children rushed to see the spaceship in the playground._

6. The woman looked out at it all. _The Princess looked out of the window at the busy market._

7. Explain how you made the sentences more interesting. _by adding more details_

Proofread the text and write it correctly.

8. two mouses appeared squeak squeak they said _Two mice appeared. "Squeak, squeak!" they said._

9. help screamed Jo climbing on the chair _"Help!" screamed Jo, climbing on the chair._

10. felix the cat creeped closer. _Felix the cat crept closer._

Remind the pupil to complete Section 3 of the Progress chart on page 46 of the workbook.

X DEFINITIVE ANSWER   X SAMPLE ANSWER

43

Schofield & Sims English Skills 2

Section 3 Writing task assessment sheet: Adventure story

Name		Class/Set	
Teacher's name		Date	

Sentence structure and punctuation

	Always/often	Sometimes	Never
Develops ideas through simple, compound and some complex sentences			
Uses a range of conjunctions to develop ideas within a sentence			
Varies sentence openings (e.g., starting with a conjunction or connecting phrase)			
Varies sentence length			
Sentences demarcated accurately			
Exclamation and question marks used to clarify meaning			
Capital letters used for names or effect			
Commas used to mark grammatical boundaries (e.g., to separate phrases, in lists)			
Speech marks used in dialogue			
Maintains tense/person/agreement			

Composition and effect

Opens the story in an appropriate way			
The event (or events) is built up in an exciting way			
Uses appropriate story language			
Connectives used to link sentences (e.g., to signal time or place)			
Vocabulary chosen for effect (e.g., to create mood or to build tension)			
Expanded noun phrases add detail			
Powerful verbs used to make an impact			

Spelling

Vowel phonemes spelt correctly			
Compound words or words with regular syllables correct			
High- and/or medium-frequency words spelt correctly			
Words using prefixes and suffixes spelt correctly			
Verb endings (**ing** and **ed**) correct			
Spelling of plurals correct			

Writing task summary

Schofield & Sims English Skills 2

Section 3 Completed proofreading task: Letter to the head

Name	Class/Set
Teacher's name	Date

Deer mrs jenkins,
[a above Deer, M above mrs, J above jenkins]

We are riteing to tell you abowt our idea for raiseing muney to by the new
[w above riteing, u above abowt, o above muney, U above by]

playgrownd equipmunt. we wuld like to hold a plant sale. we will grow plants from
[u above playgrownd, e above equipmunt, W above we, o above wuld, W above sale/we]

seed and then sell them. if we hold the plant sale afta scool we culd sell them to
[I above if, er above afta, h above scool, o above culd]

pupuls, parents and teachas.
[i above pupuls, ers above teachas]

We think it is a reely good idea becuse we can grow the plants as part of our
[al above reely, a above becuse]

science project. we has been lerning how plants grow. we will ownly need a few
[c above science, W have above we has, a above lerning, W above we]

packits of seads, some pots and some compost.
[e above packits, e above seads]

We hopes you like our idea.
Class g
[G above g]

Proofreading task summary

Section 3 tasks summary

From: **English Skills 2 Answers** by Carol Matchett (ISBN 978 07217 1182 9). Copyright © Schofield & Sims Ltd, 2011. Published by Schofield & Sims Ltd, Dogley Mill, Fenay Bridge, Huddersfield HD8 0NQ, UK (www.schofieldandsims.co.uk). **This page may be photocopied for use within your school or institution only.**

Full list of the Schofield & Sims English Skills books

Workbooks

For Key Stage 2:

English Skills 1	978 07217 1175 1
English Skills 2	978 07217 1176 8
English Skills 3	978 07217 1177 5
English Skills 4	978 07217 1178 2
English Skills 5	978 07217 1179 9
English Skills 6	978 07217 1180 5

The same workbooks, with covers designed for older users – at Key Stage 3 and beyond:

Essential English Skills 1	978 07217 1188 1
Essential English Skills 2	978 07217 1189 8
Essential English Skills 3	978 07217 1190 4
Essential English Skills 4	978 07217 1191 1
Essential English Skills 5	978 07217 1192 8
Essential English Skills 6	978 07217 1193 5

Answers

Suitable for use with both **English Skills** and **Essential English Skills**:

English Skills 1 Answers	978 07217 1181 2
English Skills 2 Answers	978 07217 1182 9
English Skills 3 Answers	978 07217 1183 6
English Skills 4 Answers	978 07217 1184 3
English Skills 5 Answers	978 07217 1185 0
English Skills 6 Answers	978 07217 1186 7

Teacher's Guide

The **Teacher's Guide** contains the **Workbook descriptors**, **Entry test** and many other useful items suitable for use with both **English Skills** and **Essential English Skills**:

English Skills Teacher's Guide	978 07217 1187 4

Also available

Mental Arithmetic (for Key Stage 2) and **Essential Mental Arithmetic** (for Key Stage 3 and beyond) are similar in format to **English Skills** and **Essential English Skills**, providing intensive maths practice.

For further information about both series, and for details of the **I can do** teaching method, which can be used with all the books mentioned on this page, visit **www.schofieldandsims.co.uk**